Ibn Battuta Award
for Travel Literature
2003 - 2019

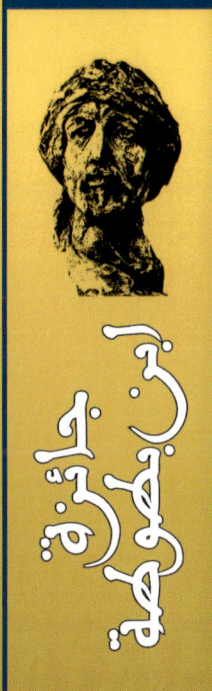

Founded in 2003, and awarded annually in the following five fields:

1- Verification of manuscripts developed in Travel Literature since the tenth century AD until the 21st

2- The best studies in Travel Literature.

3- The best book written by a contemporary traveler

4- The best book in the literature of diaries, written by Arab writers living outside their country of origin

This award has been awarded annually for 18 years. It has been awarded to more than 90 winners and they have had their books published by the Arab Centre of Geographical Literature.

The first and only prize of its kind in a long neglected field

The Arab Centre for Geographical Literature
Irtyad Al-Afaq - Venturing the Horizon

Abu Dhabi - London
E-Mail: alrihla@gmail.com

The Forum for Arab and International Relations

The Forum for Arab and International Relations cordially invites you to participate in its forthcoming international conference on

Translation and the Problematics of Cross-cultural Understanding (6)

to be held in Doha, Qatar, 7-8 December 2019.

The conference coincides with the prize-winning ceremony of

Sheikh Hamad Award for Translation and International Understanding (5)

The topics of interest include:

- The problematics of Arabic/Russian translations.

- Translation, plagiarism and the problematics of intellectual property rights.

- Translation between the accuracy of lexical/idiomatic rendering, text readability/smoothness, and target language cultural challenge.

- The problematics of translation in Islamic studies: Idioms & concepts of the cultural identity.

- Translation, dissimulation and the problematics of proscribed/taboo writings.

- The problematics of Arabic/Somali/Uzbek/Bahasa/Portuguese/Malayalam translations.

"...... and then the youngest of our foursome sisters won scholarships to attend college, books started making their way into our house. These books were like guests from a realm far removed from the world of the village, its scorching heat, and its soporific noon hours dominated by the drone of flies that served as still another manifestation of boredom and stagnation. It was a realm alien to people who praised God morning and evening for every tragedy that afflicted them, and who constantly asked forgiveness for sins they were helpless to stop committing. Books of literature, poetry and philosophical inquiry, they were guests from a world where words were laden with meanings we had never encountered before, a world of words that brought cherished hopes of justice, equality, and change for the better".

Kafa Al-Zou'bi
page 144

DIGITAL BANIPAL

Complete archive of issues for institutions and individuals

Banipal's digital edition offers readers all over the world the chance to flip open the magazine on their computers, iPads, iPhones or Android smartphones, wherever they are, check out the current issue, search through the back issues and sync as desired.

A year's digital subscription comes with full access to the full digital archive, back to Banipal No 1, February 1998 – for individuals and for institutions (based on FTE). Print and digital subscriptions are still separate for the moment.

Download the free iTunes App or get it on an Android smart-phone.

Preview the digital archive, preview the current issue or check out the Free Trial issue: *Banipal 53 – The Short Stories of Zakaria Tamer*

For more information, go to:
www.banipal.co.uk/subscribe/digital/

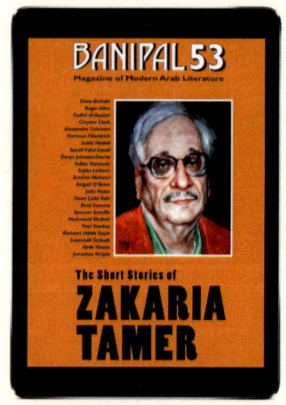

Free trial issue

Subscribe Directly to Digital Banipal
Individual: exacteditions.com/banipal
Libraries: institutions.exacteditions.com/banipal

- The contributions of Arab translators to the modern Arab Renaissance and their role in promoting multiculturalism, democracy and human rights in the Arab world.

- The overriding significance of corpus-based contextual dictionaries (II).

- Translators, academics, researchers and interested people are all welcome to apply.

- Please send an abstract (maximum 1000 words in Arabic or, if absolutely impossible, in English) summarizing the problem and methodology of the paper by 31 October 2019.

- The Conference Reading Committee will select the approved abstracts and notify the concerned participant(s).

- It is preferable to receive the approved paper in full at least a fortnight before the start of the conference, but it is possible to submit the paper in its final form after the conference (not later than 30 January 2020).

- Arabic is the official language of the conference (with English translation where necessary).

- All submissions must be made by e-mail to the following address: translation@fairforum.org

- For further information please visit our website at (www.fairforum.org) or contact the conference secretariat at (00974) 4408-0461

- The conference provides return tickets and full board accommodation.

The Saif Ghobash Banipal Prize
for Arabic Literary Translation
2019 Annual Lecture

Hanan al-Shaykh: My travels through Cultures, Languages and Writing

From Abu Nuwas to Bint Al-Shaykh

Photo: Mick Lindberg

7pm, Thursday, 7 November 2019
Knowledge Centre, British Library
96 Euston Road, London NW1 2DB

In this lecture the internationally acclaimed Lebanese novelist and playwright discusses her writing and how it continues on the path of ancient Arabic literary traditions and the great 8th-century poet Abu Nuwas in being open and bold in tackling subjects such as sexuality and feminism and has created new encounters with modernity and diversity.

Hanan Al-Shaykh is an award-winning novelist, playwright, journalist and storyteller, renowned for laying bare the world as she sees it, devoid of clichés and stereotypes. Though her works feature female protagonists who struggle to be free of social, patriarchal and religious restrictions, she never labels herself an "Arab feminist writer". Her works have been translated into 21 languages around the world. Hanan Al-Shaykh holds an Honorary Doctorate in Humane Letters from the American University of Beirut, and in June this year was made a Fellow of the Royal Society of Literature.

Tickets from www.bl.uk/events/
Full Price: £13.00 • Senior 60+: £11.00 • Student: £6.50 • Registered Unemployed: £6.50 • Disabled: £6.50 • 18-25: £6.50 • Under 18: £6.50
Enquiries: +44 (0)1937 546546 and boxoffice@bl.uk

Banipal Trust for Arab Literature, 1 Gough Square, London EC4A 3DE
Email: info@banipaltrust.org.uk Web: www.banipaltrust.org.uk

CARCANET

REBUILDING BABEL SINCE 1969

'It is impossible to imagine literary life in Britain without Carcanet.'

WILLIAM BOYD

50 YEARS OF CARCANET

Yasmeen Hanoosh

Abdelkader Benali

Abdel Aziz Jassim

Samer Abu Hawwash

Monir Almajid

11	**EDITORIAL**
12	Yasmeen Hanoosh: *The Land of Accursed Bounties, Stories from The World of Iraqi Plants*, translated by Jonathan Wright
29	Abbas Beydoun: An excerpt from the novel *Autumn of Innocence*, translated by Jonathan Wright
38	Abdel Aziz Jassim: *Three Poems*, translated by Anton Shammas and Khaled Al-Masri
48	Ahmad Abdulatif: A chapter from the novel *Elias*, translated by Robin Moger
62	Samer Abu Hawwash: "That isn't the way to make pizza" and other poems, translated by Raphael Cohen

73	**TRAVELS**
	Five tales of travel
74	Farouk Yousif: *A Poet in New York*, translated by Chip Rossetti
92	Hassouna Mosbahi: *Escape to Andalusia*, translated by William M Hutchins
104	Abdelkader Benali: To *Tangier with Emmanuel*, translated by Suzanne Heukensfeldt Jansen
118	Monir Almajid: *A Syrian Japanophile*, translated by Samira Kawar
130	Said Khatibi: *Sarajevo*, translated by Paul Starkey

CELEBRATING KAFA A-ZOU'BI
- 144 A feature on the Jordanian author
- 146 Kafa Al-Zou'bi – *Literary Influences: The Bag of Wheat*, translated by Nancy Roberts
- 160 Kafa Al-Zou'bi : The First Night, a chapter from the novel *Cold White Sun*, translated by Adam Talib
- 169 Fadia Faqir reviews *Shams Baidha' Baridah* (*Cold White Sun*)

GUEST WRITER
- 176 Linda France: *Profile and Four Poems*

Linda France

BOOK REVIEWS
- 185 Hassan Abdulrazzak: *Sentence to Hope: A Sa'dallah Wannous Reader*
- 192 Susannah Tarbush: *The Fetishists: The Tuareg Epic* by Ibrahim al-Koni
- 198 Stephanie Petit: *Printed in Beirut* by Jabbour Douaihy
- 202 Hannah Somerville: *The Clothesline Swing* by Ahmad Danny Ramadan
- 206 Becky Harrison: *The Book of Collateral Damage* by Sinan Antoon
- 210 Clare Roberts: *Celestial Bodies* by Jokha Alharthi
- 214 Shadi Rohana: *Palestine +100*, edited by Basma Ghalayini

Farouk Yousif

BOOKS IN BRIEF
- 218 *The Quarter* by Naguib Mahfouz

  The Old Woman and the River by Ismail Fahd Ismail

  A Map of Absence: An Anthology of Palestinian Writing on the Nakba, edited by Atef Alshaer

  The Book of Disappearance by Ibtisam Azem

  The Sea Cloak and Other Stories by Nayrouz Qarmout

  Modern Sudanese Poetry: An Anthology, translated & introduced by Adil Babikir

  Incomprehensible Lesson by Fawzi Karim

  Bitter English by Ahmad Almallah

  Baghdad, Adieu, Selected Poems of Memory and Exile by Salah Al Hamdani

  The Trace of a Smile by Mbarek Sryfi

Ahmad Abdulatif

- 222 **CONTRIBUTORS**

Hassouna Mosbahi

Said Khatibi

BANIPAL
Magazine of Modern Arab Literature

PUBLISHER: Margaret Obank

EDITOR: Samuel Shimon

CONTRIBUTING EDITORS
Fadhil al-Azzawi, Peter Clark, Raphael Cohen,
Bassam Frangieh, Camilo Gómez-Rivas,
William M Hutchins, Adil Babikir, Imad Khachan,
Khaled Mattawa, Clare Roberts, Mariam al-Saedi,
Anton Shammas, Paul Starkey

CONSULTING EDITORS
Etel Adnan, Roger Allen, Isabella Camera d'Afflitto,
Humphrey Davies, Hartmut Fähndrich, Ibrahim Farghali,
Naomi Shihab Nye, Nancy Roberts, Susannah Tarbush

EDITORIAL ASSISTANTS: Rosie Maxton, Annamaria Basile and Stephanie Petit

COVER PHOTOGRAPH: Abdelkader Benali

LAYOUT: Banipal Publishing

WEBSITE: www.banipal.co.uk

EDITOR: editor@banipal.co.uk

PUBLISHER: margaret@banipal.co.uk

INQUIRIES: info@banipal.co.uk

SUBSCRIPTIONS: subscribe@banipal.co.uk

ADDRESS: 1 Gough Square, London EC4A 3DE

PRINTED BY Imprint Digital, Exeter, EX5 5HY

Photographs not accredited have been donated, photographers unknown.

This issue: *BANIPAL 66 – Travels*
This selection © Banipal Publishing.
All rights reserved.
This issue is ISBN 978-1-913043-03-2.
RRP £10, €12, US$15

No reproduction or copy, in whole or in part, in the print or the digital edition, may be made without the written permission of the publisher.

BANIPAL, ISSN 1461-5363, is published three times a year by Banipal Publishing, 1 Gough Square, London EC4A 3DE

www.banipal.co.uk

Banipal magazine, founded in 1998, takes its name from Ashurbanipal (668–627 BC), the last great king of Assyria and patron of the arts, whose outstanding achievement was to assemble in his capital Nineveh, Mesopotamia, from all over his empire, the first systematically organised library in the ancient Middle East. The thousands of clay tablets of Sumerian, Babylonian and Assyrian writings included the famous Mesopotamian epics of the Creation, the Flood, and Gilgamesh, many folk tales, fables, proverbs, prayers and omen texts.

Source: Encyclopaedia Britannica

EDITORIAL

In recent years there has been a marked growing interest in translating and publishing Arabic literature in English. Those in the field have also observed that being in English translation has helped works arrive in other languages too, in effect influencing the translation of literature from Arabic into many other languages. It is a decidedly encouraging development. The viewpoint from Arab countries, however, is rather different, with many authors and critics believing that what is being translated into other languages from Arabic is not the "real" literature and, hence, not the literature that "should" be translated. The books to translate are chosen because they have won a literary prize, or because the works "suit" western readers, is what is believed. And it is a very strong belief. Of course, western publishers have their ideas about literature, their own tastes, their publishing agenda and programmes. Publishing is a commercial industry, from the biggest conglomerate to the smallest independent outfit, and it caters for an infinitesimal number of diverse readers. At *Banipal* we are very happy to see this welcome increase in works translated as we continue doing what we started 22 years ago – following the Arab literary scene as to what is being written, discussed and published, and trying to reflect that in the *Banipal* issues. Although we are mindful of what is translated, and review as many as possible, our interest is in Arab literary creativity. In this issue we publish poems by two outstanding poets, who are considered the most important voices in Arabic poetry today, the Emirati Abdel Aziz Jassim and the Palestinian Samer Abu Hawwash. Then there are excerpts from two excellent novels, *Autumn of Innocence* by Abbas Beydoun, so well known for his poetry, who in recent years has turned to writing novels, and the critically acclaimed *Elias* by the talented Egyptian author Ahmad Abdulatif, who promises the reader 'a fresh vision of history'. The main feature, TRAVELS, presents works by five innovative and established authors: the Iraqi poet and writer Farouk Yousif, writing lyrically about his journey to New York, following the steps of Federico García Lorca (part of a forthcoming Arabic book); the Tunisian writer Hassouna Mosbahi, who writes about his "Escape to Andalusia" after living in cities such as Paris and Munich; the Algerian writer Said Khatibi, with an excerpt from his book *The Inflamed Gardens of the East*, that won the 2015 Ibn Battuta Award for Travel Literature; Abdelkader Benali, the Moroccan-Dutch writer, contributing an adventurous short story "To Tangier with Emmanuel", that starts out being about 'Literature with a capital L'; and introducing Monir Almajid, the Syrian Japanophile, who has lived in Denmark since the mid-1980s but travels almost every year to Japan. In our second feature, readers will discover the exceptional novelist from Jordan, Kafa Al-Zou'bi, through a passionate and empathetic essay on her life and literary influences, and a review of and translation from her latest novel *Cold White Sun*. In this issue we also continue our Guest Writer series with the British poet Linda France, whose featured poems were inspired by a recent literary residency in Jordan. Finally, the issue opens with 'a lovely surprise', that is, stories from Yasmeen Hannoosh's *The Land of Accursed Bounties: the World of Iraqi Plants*, a 'remarkable' experimental novel in which plants are the narrators. A massive thanks to the authors, translators and editors who have made this issue possible.

YASMEEN HANOOSH

EXCERPTS FROM

The Land of Accursed Bounties:
Stories from the World of Iraqi Plants

TRANSLATED BY JONATHAN WRIGHT

> *And so He causes plants to grow for you — olives, dates, grapes and all kinds of fruit. That is indeed a sign for people who reflect*
> Qur'an 11:16

Liblab/Philodendron

I'm a frame. People like you are fond of framed stories, so I've come to bundle up the plants for you as a variety of stories in a wonderful bouquet from which you can choose what you like. Read them in chronological order as written by human hand, or rearrange them by the environment in which each plant has arisen, or pull them up by the roots and replant them some other way. Do what you like. I don't have a particular literary technique, so I won't say what course your thoughts should take.

I'm not the frame story, but rather the frame of the story. I'm a frame in the visual sense, but I'm not a decorative miniature that symbolises nature without copying it. No, I am nature itself in its truest form. I'm more like free-thinking Qashani or Fatimid decoration than Abbasid decoration, which is restrained and detached from life. I didn't come here to exclude living beings or merely allude to them. On the contrary, I have come to make them speak for themselves. I haven't come to fulfil the conventions, but rather to do away with them.

YASMEEN HANOOSH

I'm an actual frame of climbing philodendron. My stems are delicate and cannot stand on their own. So I haven't come to you with my personal story. I cling to other plants and wrap myself around whatever stories I come across, providing them with conceptual unity. I outline them with my symmetrical frame, which in its tender-skinned beauty resembles the frameworks of sacred books with gilt corners. My flowers are purely botanical, without any figurative significance. The bud of one of them connects the two halves of the opposing stems in the middle. My leaves lie on top of each other and wrap around the book and frame it page by page. They shine and give the pages a feminine allure like that of Scheherazade.

A Lovely Surprise and a Unique Experiment

A pleasant surprise that sheds light on a unique and forward-looking experiment in the realm of Arabic literature, Yasmeen Hanoosh's *The Land of Accursed Bounties: Stories from the World of Iraqi Plants* introduces us to a writer who has burst onto the literary scene with boldness and awareness through a remarkable, little precedented venture.

Hanoosh's book does not fall directly within the genre of eco-literature that has gained popularity worldwide, particularly since the worsening of environmental crises to the tipping point, since it appears to have no moral or didactic aim to speak of. Rather, it simply enters the world of literature, and of story-telling in particular, through the door of plants on the levels of both imagination and creativity. In these narrative portraits, Hanoosh casts trees and other plants in the role of story-teller. In so doing, she gives them the opportunity both to be their "plant selves," and to perform the role of the author, who recalls parts of her past and her childhood haunts in the plants' voices.

Suffice it to enumerate the plants and trees whose names the stories bear for readers to find themselves immersed in a world reminiscent of Paradise, not the Paradise from which Adam and Eve were driven after committing the primal sin as in the biblical myth but, rather, a paradise at once inhabited and abandoned, where the evil and the righteous come face to face.

ABDO WAZEN
LEBANESE POET AND LITERARY CRITIC

Imagine me wrapping myself around the rope of your thoughts with my aerial roots, which lead you to a new rhythm of breathing. Imagine my soft branches twisting and with the shadow of their heart-shaped leaves adding ideas associated with warmth and shared meaning to the stories, taking you to a new level of comprehension. Imagine me around the border in front of you, to right and to left, above and below. Then look inside me. You'll see that every story has a plant and every plant has a story. There you have only to give free rein to your wild imagination, and then you can interpret things from the perspective of the plants.

Subbair / Cactus

We are all moving targets, ceaselessly pursued by death. We spend our lives playing hide-and-seek with death until, in the end, it corners us. The game always ends in death's favour.

I hold my ground. What's the point of running away from what's inevitable? I have applied my exemplary patience to this simple concept of life. Even the most heedless of humans has not failed to notice this, and since that time I have borne a name that suits me perfectly: *sabbar*, the patient one, or, as the people in the borderlands usually call me, *subbair*, in honour of my worldly-wise patience. I tolerate the barren land and long periods of drought, and I give shelter to frightened birds and spiders. Ascetics try to emulate my patience, and those who lose their way in the desert seek out my kindness and the moisture in my flesh and my roots. My forefathers are said to have been brought from Sudan, but I have spent all my life on the borders of Iraq. Someone fearful planted me close to the artificial border in that corner where the barbed-wire fence turns north towards the arid desert, bidding farewell to the generous river and the greenery that adorns its banks. I steal a glance south from the spot where the barbed wire and my own thorns converge. In silence I gaze at the river and at the river people, who take passengers on rowing boats from the desert where I live to the wooded village of Jaykur. They planted me here because they wanted additional spikes to make sure they didn't lose the borders they had drawn for us by force. That was in the days when the people on the border fought at regular intervals, before the strangers came and dug wells for the precious poison and before the evil ones among them planned to put an end to the end of any war.

I grew up and flourished fifty or so years before the outbreak of the Third World War, or what was known as the Nuclear War, when nuclear fission wreaked massive destruction on humans, plants and animals, and not just in my desert where there are few forms of life, but over vast areas where in the past there had been thick forests, fertile hills and verdant valleys where animals of all kinds grazed.

That was when the Orange Man ruled the lands in the far northwest. It was said that madness had afflicted his mind since childhood and that he no longer had any self-respect. He became obsessed with destroying everything on the face of the earth throughout this ephemeral world of ours.

I used to watch the little boats docking at Barrak port and departing. People would come by and tell me stories, sometimes in Farsi and sometimes in Arabic. Sometimes they would talk excitedly and mix up the two languages. In the old days humans with injuries would use my refreshing sap as medicine and relieve chronic sores with it. But now my isolation is indescribable. All the humans in this country died after the nuclear bomb incident. It wiped them out, along with the birds, the animals and the creatures under the sea. The water they drank was polluted. The mullet, butterfish and herring that they used to fish with nets were poisoned. Only we cactus remained, here and there. Some of us perished with the other forms of life. Most of us turned sterile. We are trying, with great difficulty, to disperse the seeds that we have left. The few seedlings that germinate are frail and misshapen, and do not look like us at all. Their pains come with them from birth. Why do we struggle to stay alive in a lifeless world, I wonder.

Shalamcheh, 2020

Balluta/Oak

I am an elderly tree with a sturdy frame. I've seen what I've seen in the way of injustice, oppression and tyranny over the centuries I've lived on this hill overlooking the valley of silence. I don't want to bore you with the details of my private life, because it's as monotonous as the lives of all long-lived creatures that cannot move. Despite my remarkable size, most of the stories that have come my way are not much different from those that similar trees have heard in this remote rural region. But today I want to let you in on one story that turned my life into a hell from which there was no return and that made me hate men and their machines and what they do to others and to the earth, including that farmer who planted me and has fed and pruned me since my branches were tender.

I want to tell you the story of a young woman called Ghanima, or 'Trophy'. I picked up the name of this woman with a sad yet angelic face from the farmer who became her master and oppressor. She came when he called her and fell silent when he beat her. Ghanima never spoke her name to me but she told me her story during her final hours under my dense foliage, when the gallows rope hung from the thickest of my branches, waiting to be knotted around her thin bruised neck. I am only the messenger and Ghanima never shared with anyone else the horrors that I convey from her to you. Or won't you listen?

She said they marched her and thousands of other young women until three years later they reached our house. The terrorist organisation had abducted her family, who had been trying to run away from them and so could not protect her. They had killed the menfolk, and the women and girls were weakened by thirst and the ordeal of trying to escape across rough terrain. While on their way from Mount Sinjar to the west of Mosul to capture more women, the men in the organisation took turns raping her and the other women in the group. Then they sold them to slave traders, who traded women, children, slaves and similar human "resources" who could no longer speak for themselves, in exchange for hard currency or for the goods of this transitory world. In turn the brokers continued in the same manner to violate the bodies of these angelic women in the time available between obtaining them and selling them back to their relatives for exorbitant sums. Some of them went back to their distraught families. Some were killed and others committed suicide. In Ghanima's case, no one came to save her. For months various men took turns buying or selling her body or donating her to various jihad purposes. Then came the turn of my poor farmer, who paid a pittance for her battered body, as wasted as an old moth-eaten garment.

One day he brought Ghanima back with him from the village market. He presented her, bound at the wrists, as a servant for his wife, who had long complained of overwork and loneliness after her four sons had been killed in war. Her daughter had died too, possessed by some evil spirit that had driven her mad, although her father had tried by all means known to man to drive out the spirit that possessed her. The husband and his wife soon shared Ghanima between them. At dawn the wife kicked her awake to make her feed the animals and do the most arduous household chores. In the evening the husband came home from the fields and ate his meagre dinner flanked by the two women. After dinner he pulled Ghanima by the arm or ordered her to follow him to the sleeping corner so that he could mount her. Every evening the wife waited in the animal pen with the livestock until the ritual was over and her husband allowed her to come back in. Then the two women swapped places until dawn the next day. This went on for several months, and eventually Ghanima's belly began to swell. One cloudy autumn evening, after mounting her sore arse three times in succession, much as he used to mount the ewe that died right in front of him near my trunk shortly before Ghanima arrived, the farmer took Ghanima out to my place instead of the stable. He put her on the same spot where the ewe had died. His wife helped him tie her by the ankles and the neck and wrap the rope around one of my high branches. They left her there shivering the whole night long, while she told me long stories that tried my patience and endurance to the limit.

In the morning my farmer and his wife woke up and came with wicker baskets full of stones. They had chosen large stones from the remains of the ancient temple of Lalesh, which I gathered was demolished by the black organisation in the previous year. As the distant sun reached its zenith in the firmament, the villagers gathered around Ghanima. They started stoning her as she screamed. She turned to me for protection, and all I could do was soothe her fear instinctively with my rough bark, but woe is me! How could I protect her? They kept pelting both of us with rocks, howling "Whore! whore!" like jackals.

When they had vented their anger and run out of stones, they went back to their daily chores in the fields and at home. She lay close to me, unconscious, and then they came to take her pulse. When they realised that Ghanima and her unborn child still had a pulse of life, they tied her up again, and this time they tied the end of the rope to the neck of a poor emaciated cow. They pushed the cow and denounced Ghanima as a whore and a devil worshipper. They dragged the cow along the ground until its teats oozed milk and Ghanima was hanging upright alongside my trunk. The sight horrified me, as did the breeze that blew cruelly between my trunk and her listless body. The divine light inside her was extinguished for ever. If the winter hadn't already stripped me bare, I would have rustled my leaves at that moment in mourning for Ghanima. They left her there in the winter silence until the eagles finally came to finish off what remained of her memory.

Woe is me! You are gone, Ghanima, but the scar the rope left on my branch is there to this day. It haunts me and reproaches me. There is no escape from it or from the accursed memory of trees. Whenever pigeons lands on one of my branches, I complain to them, saying: "I wish I hadn't lived long enough to have my body turned into a gallows for Ghanima."

Al-Sheikhan, 2017

Zaytuna / Olive Tree

Peace be upon you, and blessed be your sacred fruit at all times. That's how they taught me to greet every newcomer. I'm a *zaytuna*, an olive tree, but I'd prefer you to call me by my original name, *zaytuni*, like Elias who has tended me, and not by the local name, *zaytuna*, which our neighbour Father George gave me – some of my branches hang over the wall of his little church, part of the monastery where gangs of barbarians with black banners arrived a week ago, intent on demolishing it.

I know my story by heart: my grandfather came to these hills seventy years ago when he was still a young seedling. Elias, the old man in whose back garden I have grown all my life, had brought my grandfather with him from a small olive-growing village on the sea many miles from here. It's said to be wonderfully beautiful, with a mild climate and some of the most delicious soil that trees have ever tasted. It has also been said that the village has been destroyed, its olive farmers killed and the women who made *zaatar* there raped. The men and women who survived dispersed across the world and spent the rest of their lives as refugees.

So my grandfather was a refugee like Elias, who escaped by the skin of his teeth with my grandfather as a cutting. My parents and siblings and I have never had a chance to visit our forefathers' country. In my childhood, when I begged my grandfather to take us back to our country, he would rebuke me harshly and then console me gently, saying: "You should thank God for your survival. If it hadn't been for that long journey eastwards in search of tolerable exile in the safe land of palm trees, we would have fallen into the hands of the foreign occupiers and we would have ended up in a kibbutz or sharing an orchard with a whole range of invasive trees brought from all the continents in the world – trees that have come to crowd us out, even uproot us, trees that have nothing to do with us or with our long history in the soil of our country."

I don't know. I haven't met these bad plants to have a personal opinion about them. And sometimes I wonder whether that fate would have been worse than what has happened to us and the people in the monastery since the fundamentalist killers arrived.

As for Elias, he avoided talk about my origins, and when people asked him where he got me from, he would answer playfully: "It's a blessed tree, an olive that's from neither the East nor the West."

He prefers being alone with me to chatting with the kind villagers. He sits under the meagre shade of my branches from time to time when the other villagers leave, and he weeps. He says my village has been wiped off the map and his land, my home, no longer exists (but how can land disappear?). He thinks back to my forefathers, who were burned one by one, and starts to sob. "It wasn't their fault, so why did they set fire to them?" he wonders tearfully. "What did the olive trees do to you, for you to set fire to them?" He converses with the absent enemy and then with me. He knows all our names and says we belonged to his forefathers who are buried there. He says the land has belonged to us and to his forefathers since eternity although the land and the olive groves have now been appropriated and destroyed.

He leaves the television blaring inside and comes outside to confide in me. He mourns his stolen past but doesn't care about the things they are stealing from us here today. He doesn't seem able to handle a second calamity, even if every aspect of it is part of his daily life. His first ordeal has completely dominated his thoughts and the pall it casts has inured him to all subsequent disasters.

Sometimes Elias's nostalgia for his homeland fills me with despair and despondency. I've never seen the land he talks about and I don't think I ever will, although the climate there, according to Elias, would suit me much better than here. I don't know my forefathers who make him cry and I have no tangible or material connection with them. I have a sense of them only through stories. He adjusts his position on his small stool and spells out his thoughts, as if speaking to himself: "Although everyone toiled and laboured, and in the end they could hardly eke out a living for themselves and their children, life was easier, more dignified, and more pleasant."

How hard it is to live in exile, and to live in a host country that is now divided. Unlike Elias, I don't have a key to my old home. I don't even have memories of my original home. My new home is not a home: nobody wants me here. They said the tyrant who once ruled them treated us as honoured guests while he wrought destruction on the people of his own country. Then they said we were working for other powers. Then they said we didn't belong because our religion was different. If I were a human being, I would say: "I have no faith or allegiance to anyone else, so leave me alone and go to hell."

After Sunday mass every week Father George waves meekly at Elias and asks after his health across the wall. In the weeks before Easter he brings children to the orchard and they start cutting off my lower branches to decorate the walls of the church, and they pray to the Virgin while breathing in the scent of my leaves. And on Palm Sunday, which they call *Ahad al-Sa'aneen* here instead of *Ahad al-Sha'aneen*, he starts bringing them early in the morning and says to them: "Take branches from this olive tree and you'll be blessed because the tree has come from the land of Jesus." Then he has them sit cross-legged in a circle around me, says nice things about me and tells them Bible stories about olives. "Christ's brow was anointed with oil. That's how his disciples could tell him from other people who were frauds and imposters." When he notices that Elias is eavesdropping on his conversation with the children, he continues: "And in the Book of Exodus olive trees like Elias's tree are mentioned when God addresses Moses and says: 'Command the people of Israel to supply you with the purest olive oil. Do this so the lamp will keep burning.'"

Sometimes the priest notices that Elias is annoyed to hear these quotations, so he suddenly moves on to tell another Bible story about olive trees. "It was Jesus who called it *muraaq* oil and that's why virgins loved it."

Father George finishes his lesson on olives, takes the children away and heads off after asking after my health and the food that Elias gives me. He pats Elias's arm and quotes one last biblical passage on olives before saying goodbye: "Remember, Elias, what Moses said: 'When you harvest your olives, don't pick them all. Leave some on the tree for the poor and for birds and wild animals.'"

To tell the truth, Elias has never denied me my due. He looks after me as if I were his daughter. He provides fertiliser and water, and makes sure I have light, shade, stories to hear and clean surroundings. He harvests my olives very carefully and makes the most delicious pickles from them in the village. He dries and crushes the stones and feeds them to the chickens, who find them delicious. He's famous for his special recipe and the village women seek him out because of it. Even so, although he generously explains his recipe every harvest season, my barrels of olives are still said to be the most delicious in the village, in fact in all the villages on the plain.

Sometimes, after a morning of arduous work around me, Elias picks up his rusty key, presses it hard against his cheek and cries. He wants to go back. Why not? Doesn't he have the key to his house? I say this even though I know deep in my roots that if he went back he would abandon me. He would leave me here in this harsh land. Sometimes, in a sweet melodic tone, he says we will both go back one day. He says that a nightingale spoke to him about it, though I haven't seen any nightingale in this garden and I've spent most of my life here. I spend much more time here than he does. Though I may be wrong, sometimes I wonder whether the right to return is all one of mankind's many lies. I also wonder whether he is trying to fool me or fool himself.

Alqosh, 2015

YASMEEN HANOOSH

Razqiyya / Arabian Jasmine

Spring hasn't started yet. Everything around me is in midwinter slumber. For some reason, I alone woke up on the archway and one of my little buds opened when we were still in the midst of winter. He noticed me immediately. He was coming out of his house on tiptoes in the morning twilight. He glanced at me dreamily as he looked up at the sky and shut the door behind him. He bowed his head and threw a glance at the windows of the house to make sure his father was still asleep. He wouldn't dare pluck me in the presence of his father, who had warned all his family not to go near his flower bushes, especially the arch of Arabian jasmine, my arch, which adorns the tall metal gate. He had forbidden them to pluck the fragrant white flowers that he cherished above all else.

He plucked me and ran off with a leap and a bound. He headed towards the side street with me in his hand, my scent flying free like teenage libido, drifting from one towering eucalyptus tree to another. He had his school books in his other hand and could hardly hold them in a bundle. He slowed down as he moved away from his father's house and approached the end of the neighbourhood. He filled his lungs with my fragrance, closed his eyes dreamily for a moment, then quickly stuck me behind his ear and set off for school. I examined the face just beside me. He had soft cheeks on which the downy hairs of manhood had hardly sprouted, a lover's face with a broad, optimistic smile, and temples wrapped in the pall of passion that had dominated his thoughts for the several weeks since he had seen a certain girl crossing the street for the first time.

He saw her coming towards him from the distance. He slowed to a halt in the middle of the narrow lane. A kerosene cart came along, pulled by a donkey and driven by a boy of a similar age. He stepped back towards the wall of a house abutting the street. They glanced at each other, then looked towards the girl coming towards them. The scene appeared to make perfect sense to the three of them. He pretended to be busy with his books until the cart moved on and left the lane. He welcomed his beloved by leaping off the narrow pavement into the street. He pulled me from behind his ear, his heart racing. It was pounding, as if it wanted his ribcage to split open so it could rush on towards her. He stood pinned to the spot. He took me by the stem and held me against his heart with exaggerated tenderness. The schoolgirl came closer. He followed her with eyes melted by passion and she threw him a half-smile, then looked down at the ground, observing the protocols of modesty and the prevalent rituals of adolescence.

She didn't look in his direction but he knew she could see him out of the corner of her eye. He raised his arms to the sky like someone appealing to some divine power, and then sniffed my flower in front of her. The girl, aware of the conventions, understood from his affected gestures that she was the flower he wanted to smell and embrace. In the language of flowers that everyone masters, she understood that he wanted to breathe deep her most intimate fragrances and hug her tight. So she walked on flirtatiously, pretending to ignore the situation, though in fact she had butterflies and birds fluttering in her stomach and her head floated in a haze of love that swore eternal loyalty to her unnamed lover. He followed her with his eyes until she disappeared and then buried his nose in my petals, accepting my readily available fragrance as a substitute for the fragrance she denied him. His ardent desire persisted. He ate some of my aromatic leaves, then stuck me behind his ear again and continued walking towards school.

He knew it was a decisive day in his life, but he had misconstrued the significance of the day.

He walked through the perfume market to the Qishla area, then his route twisted and turned as he followed his dreams. He wandered along the lanes of the Torah and Taht al-Taqiya districts. He kept on walking towards the Hannoun market and then the Christian Quarter, although his real destination was just the new bridge, which wouldn't have been far from the garden where he picked me if he hadn't meandered so much on his love journey.

I saw him walk aimlessly and I imagined the thoughts and feelings mixed up in his love-struck mind. I imagined my fragrance taking him back to childhood memories that would gladden his heart in their turn with a deep sense of belonging to this place. The bridge loomed in the distance and he suddenly recalled the early stages of its construction. He had been a child in the first year of primary school, about eight years earlier, when the city council began planning to build it. His father used to take him on short walks to watch the building process. They were both equally enthusiastic about it.

He walked on slowly towards the bridge, with images of the past mirroring expectations of a brilliant future in his mind. Time passed but he didn't notice. He pulled me out from behind his ear and stopped when he reached the middle of the bridge. It was almost half past nine. Sometimes he twirled my stem between his index finger and his thumb, and sometimes he lifted me to his nose to sniff my scent. He was late for his first lesson, so he decided to take his time walking and miss the whole lesson. He looked pensively towards the flowing river and the small fishing boats that plied it. He remembered the excitement he felt when his father promised to take him across the bridge as soon as the construction work was complete. He was elated as the bright morning sun started to rise on the Karkh side and poured its heat onto his head. He noticed little droplets sparkling on the surface of the water and imagined the river as the body of his beloved, naked except for the translucent sash of the current. It seemed to me that he was smiling at her and saying that he had crossed the promised bridge of childhood hundreds of times, and here he was today with an apparition of his first and last love for company. He wasn't bothered by the passage of time, and the idea of boredom never occurred to him. A scene of lovemaking played repeatedly in his overactive imagination. A group of university students went past him in what looked like a demonstration. At first he paid them no attention, but he found the sight of poets being carried on people's shoulders amusing and so watched the procession. One of them recited two lines of poetry with extreme fervour and the crowd repeated them after him:

Hail to the stones, the weapon our revolution has invented!
If tyrants take us to the right, we'll crush them,
And turn left to revolution!

Then suddenly a crowd gathered on the bridge, where previously people had only crossed it. Their numbers rapidly increased. Most of them were young people a little older than the boy I was with. People were spitting out angry slogans. The girls' perfumes mixed with my own fragrance, their bodies touched his body and brushed against my leaves, without him or them intending it. More girls headed towards the bridge in short skirts and many of them brushed against him with their sweaty, dizzying bodies in white blouses. They panted breathlessly, right into his face. His body stirred too. He wished his beloved were among them so that his body could give her his undivided attention. He wished her body would touch him instead of the bodies of these hundreds of students, if only for a moment.

And then a cry resounded from the two ends of the bridge:

Down with the Portsmouth Treaty!
Down with the Portsmouth Treaty!

Demonstrators advanced towards each other from both ends of the bridge, but then there were screams of panic when they noticed that armed police had started to seal off the bridge at the ends. Suddenly the crowd saw armoured vehicles appearing at the entrance to the bridge on the eastern Rasafa end, trying to stop the crowd marching in that direction. The crowd coming from Karkh set off towards the bridge with intent to cross it and join the masses in Rasafa, who were gathered in al-Amin Square. The two crowds were squeezed together in the middle of the blocked bridge. It emerged that the police had set up machine-gun positions on the roofs of buildings and on the minarets of mosques. There was no longer any room to move in any direction. He looked around towards the minaret of the al-Wazir mosque in Rasafa. He saw them pointing their guns at him from there. Then he looked towards the nearby Asifiya minaret and they were visible there too. He turned towards Karkh and the minaret of the Hannan mosque and saw them there. Suddenly, the bridge onto which he had walked as a free man with happy dreams turned in a prison, a nightmare with no escape. The decisive moment came quickly. He was among around two hundred young men and women who were shot at. I fell from his hand at the moment when he collapsed on to the ground and I came to rest in the triangle at the top of his legs, which had already started to stiffen. For a few minutes I could hear terrifying metallic sounds and cries of defiance in the face of death. Then red drops of blood started to run down from above towards the wilting whiteness of my petals. In them I could taste the dreams of new-fledged youth and complete ignorance about consequences.

The Martyrs' Bridge, Baghdad, 1948

YASMEEN HANOOSH

Amber/Iraqi Rice

I'm not the ambergris that comes from whales and is used in perfumery. I'm Amber, a grain of rice. In Iraqi I'm also called *timmanaya*. Near Shatt al-Mishkhab, where I was born, they called me *shilib*. They saw my fragrant flowers as a good omen and likened them to perfumes made with ambergris. If I left you to guess where I am now, you wouldn't be able to guess before the coming of the Second Republic.

Obviously I began my life on reclaimed land. They brought me by way of Najaf in a strong jute sack – as a gift to this family that would soon be struck by disaster. I sat in their damp dark storeroom, waiting for my time to come in the copper rice pot on the wood fire along with thousands of other grains of rice, but within a day I was taken away from those domestic places where rice is habitually stored and into the most horrible state of isolation, ending up in a communal grave for humans. I was put in the middle of a large car park. How did that happen, you may wonder? On the day I was cooked, as is the case at every celebration, the women and girls woke up much earlier than the men. They said their morning prayers for the feast, their minds focused on the prospect of a joyful gathering and festive encounters that might lead to love affairs or marriage. Then they gathered in the kitchen to prepare the banquet, in readiness for the bar mitzvah rituals. It was also the feast of Shavuot, so Shimon's parents decided to kill two birds with one stone. They decided to induct their son into the world of religious obligations and religious law on the same day as they celebrated the five books of the Pentateuch, in order to save on food supplies, of which the six families in the compound had few because of the continuing world war.

Tamara, Shimon's cousin, cooked me in the large pot. I cooked and the other grains of amber cooked around me. Our sharp aroma infused all the meat and spices in the dish of *tbeet*. In the meantime the men were at home, still fast asleep after the previous evening's sojourn in the Munir Tawiq synagogue, reciting Torah texts and singing feast-day anthems. At noon the family guests started to arrive. The baskets of fruit and shallow bowls of dairy products sat waiting for the evening eating rituals, and little Mariam sat close by, shooing away the flies and gnats. The banquet was almost ready and the bowl of *tbeet*, my bowl, was placed on the table close to the plates of vegetables and appetizers and the other festive dishes. Suddenly there were loud noises from the nearby houses: the screams of neighbours and the sound of bullets fired by assailants. After a discussion and debate and weeping, followed by whispers and entreaties, the men of the house shut the womenfolk and children in the basement and ran away.

I was stuck to the bottom of Shimon's holey sock as he fled the compound barefoot. The boy ran breathlessly through the lanes looking for a policeman or a Muslim who could save him and his family from the massacre. I flew along with him. I saw lines of rioters crossing from Rasafa to Karkh and from Karkh to Rasafa. Mobs laden with their plunder, some of them waving swords in the air. The crowds were chanting wildly:

Lovely Farhud! Let's have one every day!

In the evening, when the authorities had suppressed the pogrom, I found myself stuck in a horrible sticky patch on the bottom of Shimon's black sock, after expecting to climb green Mt Sinai on that festival of first fruits. They dug a hole in a piece of wasteland and buried us there, after their thirst for blood had been quenched and given way to remorse and shame.

The grave and its brick arch were demolished after everyone connected with the dead had disappeared from the country, and memory of the massacre disheartened what remained of its troubled Arab population. But I, and that ragged sock, decomposed there and from time to time more blood was shed in that same place. It was as if someone had answered an irresistible prayer and was plaguing the people of the country again and again.

Massacres are fun! Let's have one every day!

Nahdha Bus Terminal, 1941

The Land of Accursed Bounties will be
published by Banipal Books in 2020

ABBAS BEYDOUN

AN EXCERPT FROM THE NOVEL

Autumn of Innocence

TRANSLATED BY JONATHAN WRIGHT

ABBAS BEYDOUN

From Ghassan to Fouad

This is a letter I prefer to write by hand, as they used to write. We don't need to go over our relationship from the start. We grew up together as brothers under the same roof. Your father took me into his family after the disaster that struck my family. I was two years older than you, and Samia was my age. My father ran off that night and disappeared for all these years, but he has finally written to me. In his last letter he said he was coming back to see me. I'm worried and that's why I'm writing to you. You're no longer at home. Your father says I'm the only one he has now. I don't hate my father but I hardly remember him. I don't hold it against him that he strangled my mother. They say she cheated on him and he found her lover in bed with her. I don't hate my mother, either, and I don't feel she betrayed me. Sometimes the idea of a man in her bed disturbs me, but I don't hate her. Sometimes I want to discover her lover, whose name no one has ever mentioned. My father must have known him. When we meet I'll ask him. I think he's closer to me than my father and we have something in common. They say I could be the other man's son. They don't know who he is but they have plenty to say about a man they don't know. They even know how tall he was: didn't he jump from the balcony without breaking his legs? He landed on the ground safely, or else he would have been seen struggling to his feet. Why did the dog let him escape? Was it because he really was from the family, and that's why it didn't even bark at him? Is my father the only person who knows the secret? And then he disappeared straight away without saying anything? Everyone, even my uncle, your father, remained under suspicion, but everyone stayed where they were. They all stayed in the village – no one moved away. If they had really been under suspicion they would have shown a sign. My father's brother waited two years before he left for Beirut. The silence left wide scope for conjecture. They thought about the people who were closest. My father's two brothers were the prime suspects. They wanted the betrayal to come from within the family, but there was no indication that this was the case. I hated them but they kept trying to win my favour, they and their children. In the village they said they wanted me as an in-law. The most beautiful of them, my aunt Bushra's daughter Yusra, was as honest as usual about everything. She sent her youngest brother to look for me and she received me in all her finery, preparing me to be her fiancé. It's true that my uncle Adel has thought of moving into our abandoned house since the incident, but I refused and he didn't ask again. I had grown up among my cousins on my mother's side, but I didn't cut off my relations on my father's side. The only reason for this was that I believed the rumour. The dog hadn't barked, but that wasn't enough to accuse my father's brother. The dog's now tethered in the garden and I look after him. I feed him and take him for walks. He's what's left of my family. He runs ahead of me, comes back to me and runs around me. He's old now and his eyesight has started to weaken. He wasn't even a year old when my mother died. He spent days by her grave, until her brother brought him back and tied him up in the garden. Her brother wants me to leave the dog for other people to look after but I insist on doing that myself, on time, every time. I love how he barks and jumps up as soon as he notices me. He's old but he still stands up on his hind legs, licks me and runs around me. They think the dog's the only one who knows the secret. They're waiting for him to drag someone in by the shirt, or jump on someone and pin him down, but he hasn't done that. My father left him at home and disappeared.

When the woman next door found my mother strangled in bed she screamed and the neighbours flocked to her screams. My aunts and uncles on my mother's side, who lived in the same neighbourhood, also came running. My uncles on my father's side, who lived on the edge of the village, came late and were criticised for their tardiness. My father had strangled my mother and that wasn't something they could disavow. It was their brother who had done it and it wasn't easy for them to be at the scene of his crime. By daring to come, they were blaming my mother and absolving my father of his crime. They were in two minds and came at the end, when the house was full of people and it was clear that my father had got away with his deed. Even so, people condemned them for what their brother had done. They turned up with their womenfolk and their adult children and clustered in one part of the house, along a wall where a picture of my father was hanging. They let the others go in and then left. They didn't shout or raise their voices. They had come only so that they wouldn't be blamed for the crime. The police turned up from the village police station but they didn't do anything. They knew there was no longer anything they could do. Ever since the fedayeen had come into the village and many of the local youths had joined them, these matters were no longer the business of the police. They were nobody's business. My father had fled and there was no one we could look to for justice. First everyone had to be convinced a crime had been committed. My father's flight was a piece of evidence, but if he had found a man in her bed, he had a right to kill her. People knew he was quick-tempered and violent and they had often saved her from his assaults, but now it was a different matter. He had seen a man in her bed. No one was certain of this but the crime amounted to something of that kind. The crime was consistent with such an act of infidelity. The crime was evidence of betrayal. My father's relatives gathered under the picture of my father and didn't speak. No doubt

Abbas Beydoun's novel *Autumn of Innocence* explores religious extremism and a traditionally masculine society through the tragic story of a father-son relationship that comes to a head during the Arab Spring.

The book opens with a letter from the son Ghassan to his cousin Fouad describing how his father Massoud strangled his mother and then fled from his village in southern Lebanon. Ghassan was three years old and grew up stigmatized by his father's violent crime.

One day, Fouad's mother – Massoud's sister – confesses that she encouraged Massoud to kill his wife, believing that her low socioeconomic status was embarrassing their wealthy family. She also says that Massoud feared his wife would reveal he was impotent, undermining his status and sense of manhood.

Massoud moved to Syria, remarried and had two more sons. But during the Arab Spring, as militant groups fight the Syrian regime he becomes a religious extremist, and returns to his village, bringing with him a group of men. Together they take over and terrorise the village and begin murdering the inhabitants in the name of religion. A friend of Ghassan is a victim, and Massoud also threatens his family, so Ghassan decides he must kill him to avenge the deaths of his friend and the other villagers, but, instead he is killed by Fouad who had joined the extremists.

they were mulling questions of this kind. With time, no doubt the others started to ask themselves the same questions. As soon as they buried my mother they declared her guilty. The sight of her strangled in her bed was evidence against her. They had started talking about the lover's name. They didn't find a name but they guessed it was a relative, a very close relative. My father disappeared and the lover disappeared. It wasn't difficult. It happened easily and it must have happened within the family. It must have been part of a family feud, and it might have been an issue between two brothers. It might have been between cousins. It definitely didn't go further than that.

It might have been a case of a woman sleeping with two brothers in the same room and in the same bed. Of my father's two brothers they chose Omar, the younger, as the prime suspect. He was the same age as my mother, and maybe that was why they chose him rather than the elder brother, who was bigger and more handsome and, on top of that, had a big reputation with women. They chose the younger one, who seemed stupid to them and even stammered. They compared him to my father, who was big and tough and quick to draw a knife. It was said they gave my mother to my father out of fear. She couldn't refuse. He had stopped her in the street to tell her he was going to marry her. My father owned half the village. In fact his mother was the heir and the property was hers, but the man who got hold of the property automatically became village headman. My father said he was going to marry her, but my mother, who was seen as the prettiest girl in the village, raised an eyebrow and didn't answer. She didn't like him speaking to her in the middle of the street. She was with a friend and he had spoken to her in the friend's presence. He hadn't taken her aside to talk to her. He said what he said and walked on without waiting for an answer. He was just telling her. It was as good as an order. He had made the decision for her and she needed only to know. His mother didn't want him to marry her. In front of many people she said she wouldn't go down to her wretched house to ask for the hand of a shopkeeper's daughter. That would be beneath her. The village talked about it and fragments of gossip reached my mother's family. When there was too much talk of it, she couldn't take it anymore. She went to her aunt's house in Beirut and disappeared there. A week later my father followed her to Beirut and told her she had to come home. This time my mother raised an eyebrow again and said: "That's not how people get engaged." If he wanted her, he would have to stop his mother talking about her. She wasn't worthless because she was a shopkeeper's daughter. If his mother didn't feel honoured to be received in their house, there was nothing to discuss. My father was angry when he heard this but he refrained from hitting her. He did threaten her, however. If she didn't come home she would be responsible for whatever happened, he said. My mother went back to the village the same day, worried that someone might insult her father. But she stayed home and never went out. In the end my father's mother backed down, visited my mother's family and proposed the marriage. They agreed and she agreed. The visit was enough for them. No one in the village would have turned down a suitor like my father.

I wasn't yet three years old when the disaster struck. They moved me to the home of my aunt Bushra. Her house was full of children — six and now a new one that made the house even noisier, a new one who wouldn't be welcomed by the others. I kept my distance in fear but they drew me in and made me one of them. That way I became a pawn in their contests. There was room in their games for someone they could push around and sometimes slap, and I was usually that person. My aunt defended me, since I was an orphan who needed her kindness, but this made me a target for their revenge. For some reason or other I moved to the home of my maternal uncle Jawad. This came as a relief to me. You and your sister Samia were my age. In fact at the age of five I was a few days older than you two. It was as if you needed a third and were waiting for one. You took me into your lives with ease. Three children find more games than two. Your mother, who I gathered was my mother's friend, thought she had a duty to protect me. My father's sisters and brothers continued to take an interest in me and help with my education. They enrolled me in an expensive foreign school that Uncle Jawad couldn't have afforded, and where he didn't send his own sons. After that they moved me to the American University, and I was a hard-working student because no-one had ever pushed me to work hard. No-one brought me up but the street didn't take me up either. Uncle Jawad was frightened of disciplining me. He saw me as a ward that he only needed to protect and preserve. For my part, I needed to be in a family, so I had to make one. I tried to be Uncle Jawad's right hand. I saw his decisions as an obligation I had to fulfil and I tried to hold you two to them, even when they made no sense. Uncle Jawad wanted me to be friends with my cousins on my father's side. This time things didn't go easily. They weren't ready for that. I tried to force them to be friends. I waited for them in their homes but when they came home I found them indifferent towards me. The fact that my father had murdered my mother rubbed off on me. It was a legacy I couldn't shake off. I lived on the sidelines and I couldn't easily become part of the family. This stigma was like a birthmark that no one would forget, as if it had always been part of me. There was even a trace of pity or disapproval in the way other people looked at me. That was life's gift to me, roughly speaking. I had come from an act of murder, from a crime. I think I did my best to cover it up. I was always worried that something I did might suddenly call attention to it.

Eventually when I was thirteen I found my way to the mosque and I deliberately carried the Qur'an in my hand and fasted several days a month. But all that wasn't enough to reassure me. I would panic at the sight of a knife or a rope, as if they stirred memories deep inside me. When I drank my first glass of beer, I felt I was a murderer, but I insisted on drinking it. Maybe I was insisting on murdering. That night I went home very tired and fell asleep immediately. I always felt that my fingers were short because my father had put his fingers around my mother's neck. Having short fingers felt like a defect as bad as murder.

I didn't see my mother lying strangled. They stopped me seeing her. I was frightened by their rigid faces, and I didn't object. I still fault myself for depriving her of having one last look. But I gather from what my aunt Bushra said that I formed an image of a tongue hanging out from between her lips, a bruised neck, and eyes bulging from their sockets. It was an image that grew more grotesque with time, punishing me for my evasion. So I was afraid of my dead mother and afraid specifically of her death, of her lolling tongue and her bulging eyes. What I heard from my aunt Bushra about my mother, or what I gleaned from her, painted a very different image. My mother was a shopkeeper's daughter who was uppity toward her masters. She also had roving eyes that devoured men. In my presence Auntie Bushra made a point of praising my father, describing him as kind, and thereby holding my mother wholly responsible for what had happened to her. It was her crime and she had brought evil on herself. I never heard that from Uncle Jawad. As far as he was concerned my father was a monster and my mother was very beautiful, like a dove. This wasn't just what Uncle Jawad said. Many others said it in other ways. They said my father was a thug, a tyrant and as strong as a lion. Given the way he was they wouldn't rule out him hitting anyone, since that was his stock in trade. No one would be surprised if he hit out, or even if he hit a woman, since that was an aspect of hitting, and that was part of his power and his thuggery. A man like him needed a woman to submit to him and she had no right to do otherwise. They said my father was violent and quick to punish anyone who wouldn't obey him. And naturally those who didn't obey him deserved it. They had provoked his power and brought it to the surface. How much more so if they were close relatives, if it was his wife who had been disobedient? Wasn't that an insult to his power? Didn't he have to discipline her without hesitation? There were, however, people who condemned my father for killing an innocent woman, saying he had no right to kill her, even if she was spoiled and highly strung. I picked up things like this and it made me more puzzled. I didn't like my aunt Bushra or my other aunt, Khulood, or their children. I can't think of any reason why I don't like them, but I can't like them. Without taking an attitude I knew this was an atmosphere in which my mother felt stifled, and whatever the reason it was still a stifling atmosphere. I felt I couldn't find enough air to breathe there and I could sense from afar that the hatred for my mother was being projected onto me. Like her, I was weak and abandoned there. I didn't resemble her otherwise, though in the eyes of my father's relatives I was only her son. Only to some extent was I the son of my father, who had lost his home because of her and possibly because of me. They used to pick up news of him and grieve for him. The story of my mother's murder was long forgotten. Now the story was about a fugitive who roamed the hills and then went abroad. Khaled, my father's other brother, was usually the one who met him, gave him money and came back distressed. When he came back I felt hated. I didn't ask and I didn't want to know where he was or what he was doing, but Uncle Khaled passed on his regards to me anyway. I was indifferent, and this irritated my father's brothers and their families. My silence when they spoke about my father made me seem insensitive and cruel to them. They had their reasons for disliking me: I had been born in that crime, as if I were its child. The sins that we bear unintentionally are the ones that appear on our faces.

Sins can be passed on by heredity or by contagion or we may even be born with them. The more I grew up the more I was my father's son. The way they looked at my hands changed, as if they could see blood or traces of blood on them. A crime, like love, requires two people, and if the first person can wash his hands, the second cannot remove the stigma from his face or the traces of the crime from his neck. It's complicated and we can't easily understand the responses to a crime. That's why my aunts Bushra and Taghrid insisted on burying my mother in the garden of the house, and neither my father's brothers nor Uncle Jawad disagreed with them. I didn't understand why they hadn't wanted them to carry her to the cemetery, or what that had to do with the crime. Did they want the crime to stay within the house? Under the pomegranate tree they had set a marble headstone engraved with a row of arches. In front of it was a rectangle that sloped down over supports either side and ended at the foot in a low, curved marker. Beside the grave there was a basin into which water flowed from a fountain, that was surrounded by blue when the water reflected the sky. I don't know why they insisted that everything should remain on my father's land until the conflict somehow came to an end. Were they worried the funeral might bring to light things they wouldn't be able to live with? Uncle Jawad wanted to pin the crime on them but my father's sisters wanted the affair to remain within the family and to be buried with her. After that Uncle Adel had a notion that it was improper, even heretical from a religious point of view, to turn a house into a burial place. He was thinking of moving into the house, or of making use of it in some way. But my father's sisters prevented him and my mother's brother wouldn't agree to his plan. The crime lay years in the past and it was indecorous to dig it up again. Besides, the crime was still unsolved, not a closed case, and to move the body would be to repeat the crime, to put a pair of hands around her twisted neck again.

Kharif al-Bara'ah (Autumn of Innocence),
Winner of the 2017 Sheikh Zayed Book Award for Literature,
published by Dar Al-Saqi, Beirut, Lebanon, 2016. ISBN 9786144258811

ABDEL AZIZ JASSIM

Three Poems

BEFORE THE BRASS AND THE PHOTOGRAPH

1

Before the brass and the photograph, before the mills and the eulogies and the yellow fever, the world was stillborn, head severed asunder like the mouthpiece of a saxophone. Between the wrath of thunder and the wasteland of creatures, its light suddenly vanished behind the hills.

Yet, they said: a magic hand on the eastern front rescued him, stripped him of his aubergine attire and his wide, milk-white girdle, and unburdened him of the armour of conviction. She collected his trickling blood with a spoon, washed the sickle of slaughter and cleansed it of the screams, stitched up his gaping wounds and gave him back his forlorn, snowy head. Seven times she kneaded his spine till cracking of bones was heard, and rubbed the soles of his feet with a magnet, then pulled out from his mouth, ever so slowly, the rattling, long-drawn-out thread of death.

2

Before the brass and the photograph, before the mills and the eulogies and the yellow fever, Evil was born, with a thousand hearts made of stone, thumping inside his chest like mourning bells. Born in a storm of mud, between two of suicidal lightning strikes, he learnt how to urinate in mouths, creeping like serpents, glittering like tobacco tar in the marred eyes of earth.

And so, with a crown and sceptre, from the gallows hearts were hanging.

3

Evil was born, with a thousand hearts made of stone, and they made the grave climb up to us in dreams. Where could we possibly find a place to hide? And who will pull our coffins when the sword lurks over the throat of justice and our years dissolve in the cauldrons of forgetfulness?

Evil was born, and nothing will stand in his way: malice is a rumbling river of smut, and ruse is two rivers. Harm is a network of interconnected seas, and composure is nothing but an echo.

As for this mouth that's kissing us now, it might order our death tomorrow. And here are the diaper and the shroud hovering over the roofs. The door through which wet-nurses came will be the door through which women corpse-washers leave.

Evil was born the way masks are born, and here's his large flag fluttering over the relics of the world.

4

Between the brass and the photograph, between the mills and the eulogies and the yellow fever, I too was born, in a marine sunset, and they found a key etched on my chest. The arm that pulled me out of the sea, put the night's speckled beard under my head so I could watch the clear sky alone. She lifted the veil of the hawk that had flown with my umbilical cord toward the smoky mountain, covered me with amulets and named me al-Aziz, The Noble One. And then with a swift move, through which all thoughts of the universe have passed, she gouged out the eye of an ailing dawn and put it in the empty drinking cup in front of me.

Go ahead, she said, examine death with your own fingers, and don't let him scare you, because he's just a field squirrel, just an ancient bear hunter. That is your eternal shadow, under his giant turban, where salvation and life lie down together like a married couple. So don't let them slip from your grasp, and don't waste your time fighting him. The sun is your sight, its darkness is your meaning, so don't be weary of your determination, and don't lick the wine of animals lest you collapse. Don't chain your feet with defiled dust, lest you diminish and melt away and live like a mosquito.

5

Between this and that, in a timeless place, I passed through the cleft of an earthquake. Harm kept rolling over my eyelids like a needle-filled canopy. And when I reached the downslope of the sandglass, almost breathless, while the plague washing his hair between two banks and the one-legged scorpion following my footsteps, I threw everything behind me and cast a loving look at the tomb of the sea. Then I moved away, farther away than my life itself, away from offspring who do not live or die, or stranger still – do not die or live!

TRANSLATED BY ANTON SHAMMAS

ABDEL AZIZ JASSIM

FOOTPRINTS IN A MATCHBOX

"I'm vanishing, and my dust will become what I am."
Hafiz al-Shirazi

1

They arrived
and through the resurrection door
they entered.
The apple of nostalgia was shining
between their teeth
whenever lightning turned around
and knelt over their footprints.
Then, after they had dismounted
and stretched out, dead,
under the blanched palm fronds,
wolves howled in the valley
and generations sullied with venom flew
at their feet.

2

The five men, from an eternal quest they came. From the tallows of sorrow, the noses of storms. From lands scoured with dust, which travellers gasp at forever but never cross. From the firewood of hearts, with the desert a notebook of masks. From a dawn hanging by its hair, a mistake in a game of knives. From deprivation that sits cross-legged in their laps and slaps them with every moan. From the caves of sighs, with darkness a white-bearded bachelor whose dreams make widows give birth. From the silence of mountain hermits as they raise death and walk him in the streets like a wild cat. From mountaintops and corpses. From that flickering lighthouse, on and off, like a distress signal from an ever-drowning man. From the kingdoms of sun, the departures of sails. From Asia's face, overturned on a volcanic rock, to Africa's tattoo, emitting smoke between tropics – their lives tossed about back and forth, like smoke signals of Native Americans.

3

From that word engraved on horseshoes:
Exile, Exile,
Exile,
they came and passed through the hills of ashes,
chests bare,
with the wisdom that settled like the eye of a hawk
in their pockets.
Their star was bewildered,
as it landed on the saddles
and on the life ahead of them,
and then soared.
Whenever drowsiness overtook them,
and their sight began to blur,
they would tie their long beards
to the necks of their horses
and fall asleep.

4

The five men, fearlessly,
were sleepwalking,
under the crabs' purple moon
and listening to the crawling of five centuries
sobbing and groaning
beneath them.

A falconer was following them,
and when their feet,
hearts,
and nightmares
would turn red on the sand,
he would cry
 and hard rain would pour down.

ABDEL AZIZ JASSIM

5

Those men! Those men!

Fearing they would be defeated and the sign of regret
would grow bigger upon their foreheads,
they jumped onto the giant hammer,
onto the citadel of nails,
and pumped their blood
into the neck of air.

Still, after a while they reached the edge
and it was raining
when an arrow flew from the outskirts of town
and pierced one of them in the chest.
Resigned he shouted:

"Lord! How vile they are!"

Then he sat up straight, took a deep breath, bit down on his handkerchief, broke off the bloody arrow, and spat on it. He lit his pipe and his eyes clouded over as he chanted an ancient song. He wrapped his arms around his old horse's head and fell between the birds that gathered around him like a shroud of feathers.

6

The second:

As if he were dreaming,
he plucked out his heart
without spilling a single drop of blood.
He squeezed it in his fist,
like one who wants to rid himself of a deadly sensation,
until out of him came curses,
clouds,

shrapnel,
and a minecart carrying a bride
in her wedding gown sleeping
in a coffin.

7

The third:

Fidgeting,
he put his ear to the rock,
along with his life
and the old letter he never sent.

Then he heard the sound of an earthquake in the distance,
as it crossed the plain and the town,
climbed the valleys and the star,
climbed day and night,
and rang out right in the centre of his skull.

Then he rolled up his long shadow,
cleaned out his ear,
and went on to bury
the letter, torn
in his hands.

8

And the fourth:

He gazed from the top of the high hill.
He teared up
when he glimpsed his homeless childhood
carrying the barrel of orphanhood upon her back,
carrying shipyard wood and water-skins,
carrying stones and clods of mud from houses.
Then, standing nailed to the spot,

hungry,
in a threadbare dress,
sucking her salty fingers
outside the baker's window.

9

As for the fifth:

He stood up promptly,
fired an angry bullet
at the sky,
and looked around.
Then he held a picture
that still bore the warmth of his heart
lifted it up
and gasped
as he kissed it.

But, with a sudden movement,
he leapt into the deep valley,
like someone sliding down a tube,
leaving the cloak of his rebellion
hanging from a branch of the tree
overlooking
the downslope.

10

Indeed, they have finally arrived. They divided the loaf of fires between them after their limbs turned to ash and the cormorants preserved their life story.

So they have arrived, to the Paradise that once expelled them. The Paradise of locusts, and coffins, and stitched-up mouths. Like a band of lovers that love rolled down from high above, and they touched the wood of gallows tenderly with their fingers.

They have arrived, by heaven! But you, woman, were drunk in the bar of the blind for a long time, and left your eyes for the wicked woodpecker to plunder.

They have truly arrived! But having become so thin they became threads in the needle of forgetfulness.

11

Here is their theatre, their abandoned cellar, where the story is asleep:

There are footprints in a matchbox. Eyes of horses under an inverted bell. Pains dealt out and loaded into earthenware jars. A huge star amidst a pile of smut. A map with tattered edges. Candles, swords, and cobwebs. Threadbare caftans and pipes stuffed with old tobacco. Torn sandals and hats mottled with dried blood. Whips, belts, and shackles. Dusty bones and screams suspended between the jaws of skulls.

Between this and that there are on the shelf five punctured hearts in glass jars. We carried them with us and, with a sole finger, wiped the metallic falcon's rusty tear.

TRANSLATED BY KHALED AL-MASRI

From the poet's collection *Alaam Taweela ka Dhilal el-Qitaraat*
(Long Pain like the Shadow of the Trains), 2010
Poetic Works, Part 1, published by Dar al-Tanweer, Beirut, 2017

READ the third poem, also translated by Khaled al-Masri,
on the website at
www.banipal.co.uk/selections/

AHMAD ABDULATIF

Elias, my name is Elias

THE FIRST CHAPTER OF THE NOVEL *ELIAS*

TRANSLATED BY ROBIN MOGER

I'm Elias. My name is Elias. Or Elias is what they named me. Or what they claim they named me. What they think my name is. Elias. Elias is the name, the name I tell myself. I might say, for instance: Read, Elias. Elias, get dressed. Time to go out, Elias. Elias, listen to what you're told. Do the right thing, Elias. And so on constantly, without cease or stop or break. Continuously, repeatedly, relentlessly. I usually use the imperative when I speak to myself, and when the imperative comes from me, I usually don't comply. Usually – because I am Elias – I don't know myself. I don't recognise myself. I don't meet myself. Not usually. And if, by chance, I do, then I say: Elias! Seize the moment! Revel in it. Impose Elias's terms upon it. But the moment never lasts. It flits away, it melts away, and only Elias remains. Elias and I, left together forever, each issuing orders to the other, and neither doing as they're told. We fall into the whirlpool of each phrase, between the words and the letters, between the stern tone and the silence that follows the stern tone. We fall into the void, into the well. Into the unknown or into the known. We reach an accommodation: do the same things according to a routine, without thinking. That way we'll come to peace and understanding. That way we'll be friends.

My name is Elias. A Hebrew name, they say. From Eliyahu. The 's' was added in the Greek. They say it's a Muslim and a Christian name both. Of a prophet mentioned in the Torah and in the Quran. A coincidence. It's nothing more than a coincidence. I'm not a

AHMAD ABDULATIF

prophet, nor a saint, nor a righteous man. Nor sinner either, as it happens. I'm just Elias. Elias plain and simple. In some respects my life, like that of others, might intersect with the prophet's story. In some respects, like others, it might not. The prophet's life might, in some respects, intersect with others' stories, and my story play no part in it at all. Everything's on the table. All things are possible. To clarify: making connections between people on the basis that they share a name is nonsense. Babble. I say nonsense and babble, but I don't think of coincidence as nonsense and babble. Likelihood isn't nonsense. Probability isn't babble. I admit I'm fond of the name Elias. That I like anyone who bears the name. I refer here to my friends on Facebook who bear the name Elias. I don't have friends outside of Facebook. Because I don't have friends. But my friends on Facebook are called Elias. Or Umm Elias. Madame Elias. Elias plus their father's name. Or nickname. Or plain Elias. Elias they're called, and the name makes me fond: as though its letters are components in my story. Components of my history. Of my identity. My bewildered identity. My I-don't-know-what-my-identity-is identity. Like the name in the end is I. I, and I don't know who I is. I could

---

In Ahmad Abdulatif's fourth novel, *Elias*, we encounter a fresh vision of history in which the narrator shuttles between two parallel civilisations and religions, taking as his theme years of unrest and instability in Cairo and Granada. Foregoing narrative convention, with an innovative approach to time and space, he offers us a patchwork of stories about himself, Elias, a person with a unique nature and limitless potential.

The novel interrogates identity, or more exactly, the loss of identity. It is a quest for roots, mediated through a language that is effervescent and playful, weaving together its strands then pulling them apart. Through repetition and variation a singular and strange myth is constructed. Indeed, it presents us with a "new code" to govern the mechanics of language, one that is perfectly suited to our many-layered protagonist as he searches for his roots through the byzantine complexity of his tragedy, depicting a man ground down and defeated, who relishes his subservient existence in red cities ruled by tyrants, beneath whose concrete ceilings there is no space for freedom.

AMANI FOUAD, EGYPTIAN LITERARY CRITIC

be the all the Eliases in the world and not know it. One part, perhaps, of a vast and ungovernable Eliasity: fertile and proliferating. One atom, one electron. A spoke in a vast wheel. The Eliastic Wheel. Speculations which transport me to fresh fields of doubt, to a place in which I begin to doubt my own uniqueness, the closed nature of my private story, of my personal experiences. These speculations let me come to terms with myself. They give me a balm for my wounds and a rack on which to hang my sins. An ostrich-feather pillow on which to lay my sleepless eyes to rest. Every Elias has done the same, I'd say. Even the Elias-less are looking for that cure-all balsam. None of which prevents me from sympathising with other people. And none of it promotes sympathy. It accounts for nothing. For I am Elias, and that is my greatest distinction, regardless of the name's etymology and evolution in the Greek.

I am thirty years old. Forty. Seventy. Two hundred? Maybe more! Maybe less. Maybe somewhere in the middle of the ages cited. And maybe not. Maybe nothing at all: ageless. But here I am, writing and speaking in this very moment. Thinking and moving, sleeping and dreaming. I have been doing all these things for a long time. For a long time, these things have been doing me. The doing and I make the long time. That's how the relationship works, though it might not seem so: time makes me and makes the doing; the doing and I make time. Also, I make the doing and the doing makes me. Time blames me because I haven't saved it from growing old. I claim it's time who has given me the growing old. And the doing's got it worst of all, because the growing old's what stops the doing being done. It pleads with me. It says: I've given up doing. That I've run away from doing. And when it calls my name I pretend to be deaf. The doing says I didn't hold out a hand to help when doing was drowning in a deep blue sea. The doing's right. I've given up on doing hundreds of times. Haven't heeded its ringing cries. I haven't held out a hand for all that doing's sure that I could have. But what doing doesn't know is that, looked at another way, I didn't save myself. Didn't save myself when I went tumbling into the abyss. Didn't lend myself a hand. No hand of mine reached out when I was drowning. I drowned in the deep blue sea. I didn't open the door when the gas was choking me. I didn't block the bullets heading for my heart. As regularly and often as the clock's tick, death came to me, and I never stepped aside. It's not right that doing blame me. It's not right that

I blame time. Not right that time blame me. Not right that time blame doing. Nothing's right. Nothing's not. Nothing happens. Nothing should. Nothing should not. Nothing shouldn't not. So I am Elias. Because of all that, I am Elias. Because of all that, I remain Elias, and despite everything, I rejoice in my Eliasity, my own special Eliasity. It's mine, this Eliasity, and no one knows a thing about it. No one knows my Eliasity because my Eliasity knows no one. Because my Eliasity doesn't care to know anyone. And no one knows it, because they don't care to, either. All things are equal. They all go the same end. To every action a reaction equal and opposite in force. To every reaction an action equal and opposite in force. To every force an action which drops one person to the ground. To every ground a corpse laid out. To every corpse a soul which leaves it to settle in a body. To every body a life. To every life an age. And so I say: My age is thirty, forty, seventy, or two hundred. I am a son of the earth. The earth is my mother. The earth is my daughter and I am the earth's father. The earth is my stepmother and my mother's sister. My sister. Brother. Bound by blood. Bound by birth. We are siblings, so we do not hold one another to account. Like, it never tells me: Elias! Your credit in this world's exhausted! Leave! No, it's never said that. Never. It never would or could. We're bound by blood and birth and, furthermore, by friendship. The earth keeps all things safe in the belly of the earth, or in its heart. But it knows me. The earth knows me well. It knows me better than I know me. Despite the fact that no one knows me better than I do. But the earth knows me best of all. I don't like depth. And I don't care for closed-in spaces. I'm of the surface. I like to move over the skin, to hover over the breast, to brush buttocks. To push a part of me into openings, sure, but into the heart? I don't like to stay inside. So no to death. Yes to immortality. And the earth knows it. The earth knows it well, better than I do, so it spits me out like the sea spits out oil, like the sea spits boats to the shore. Or swallows them. But the earth doesn't swallow me. It knows I love the surface. It knows I'm a useless boat without an oar. Without a captain. A useless boat without a net to fish. It knows I'm Elias, and that my Eliasity prevents me doing many things. Hence doing's suffering. Hence time's complaint.

I am lonely. Very lonely. Unbearably lonely. It's not the loneliness that's unbearable, it's me. I'm unbearable because I'm lonely. It's simple. Well, not completely simple, because it's also complicated: the world drove me to loneliness, so I felt alone, felt spat out by the world, and then I was. With me, the question is which came first? A question as old as the chicken and egg. A question I won't answer honestly if asked, though the answer might surface in the story. But I don't know the story. I don't know the truth of the story. I don't know the true story. Stories surround me. Of my birth. Of my childhood. Of being a young man, and an old man. Of my death. Not to mention the stories of my resurrection. And can I say with certainty which of them took place? I cannot. I cannot say which didn't. Particularly concerning my death. My death is controversial. I have heard stories about my death, no end of stories. When will I tell my stories? Will I tell my stories? Maybe the time will never come. For every time there is a call. For every call a prayer. For every prayer a set number of rakaas. So they say and so I don't believe. But I say what they say. I repeat what they say like a parrot. Like a scholar of the faith I commit what they say to memory. Believe though? No. And maybe the time doesn't come. Maybe the ears don't hear the call. The ears, maybe, are occupied. Who can control the ears? All is chaos. Amid the chaos, you might make an order. And you might not. In any case, I know that everything comes when it comes and without anyone calling on it to come. Waiting for love doesn't bring love. Striving for happiness doesn't bring happiness.

(What's happiness, though? I don't know. Mysterious word. A word people treat like a sack of wheat. A sack of wheat they must come out of their houses to carry away from the shop on the street corner.)

Waiting for death, on the other hand, does bring death. Losing the will to live brings death. A fill of life brings death. Perhaps that's why they killed me, time after time. Killed me without me dying. Or was it that I died without me knowing. I don't know. Nor do I know what the dead feel. What they see. How they speak. Do the dead know that the dead are dead? I don't know. I do not know. But I know that I am a moving corpse. I know that I have been one since time immemorial. I know that the moving corpse walks about. It sleeps and it wakes. It eats and it shits. The corpse looks out at the world from the balcony. I know that I am a moving corpse and that I appear in the mirror like a moving corpse. But why this voice pursues me, its questions dinning in my head when I know no answers to any questions, I do not know. Though I know other things. I know women who visit the graves on Thursdays and hand out loaves to the other visitors and the Quran reciters and the guards. I know children who read Quranic verses at the gravesite because the recitation of children can reach the dead. I know men and women who lay roses on the graves. I know that the men and women do this to bring comfort to the dead inside their graves. To ease their torment. I know those who go to the graves to tell the dead about everything that is happening in life. Those who say that the dead see us though we don't see the dead. Who say the dead look out at us from behind a pane of glass and that this pane cannot be crossed. With my own eyes I have seen women in the company of children come out of their houses at dawn before the Eid prayers to visit the dead. Wrapped in black. Women who've lost their men. Lost their backs. Lost the pillars that held up their homes. Maybe in a war. Maybe in a revolution. Maybe in a civil war. A train accident, maybe. Women certain that the dead were waiting for the women. But I didn't see the dead. I didn't see the dead move. Or hear them speak. But I can't say for sure they don't. I can't be sure because I am dead and I do. I don't like to say 'dead'. I prefer: A moving corpse. A walking corpse. When it comes to the dead, movement is more accurate. Much more.

I am Elias and I own nothing of any value. I own only shelves. A set of worthless shelves. A set of shelves that house a number of notebooks. A numberless number of notebooks. Notebooks and loose pages. Worthless notebooks and loose pages. Notebooks and loose pages inscribed with the name Elias. Just the name Elias. Elias only. That worthless name. Elias and no father's name. No mother's. No description. The name Elias and a date at the end of every one. The notebooks have small pages. The other pages are loose. Loose and long. Easily folded and cut. The notebooks and the pages are here, on the shelves. On the shelves, and I don't know who put the notebooks and the loose pages on the shelves. No one knows who put the notebooks and loose pages on the shelves. I don't know when they were written. I don't know if they're mine. But the notebooks and loose pages bear my name, and my handwriting. My clear hand. The dots drawn as circles. Those pronouns for the passive that are missing in my speech. The possessive pronouns that are trying to disappear. The tanween, even as my tongue rebels against it. With commas missing. With commas sidelined. With commas even as I'm trying to sideline commas. With full-stops everywhere. With full-stops everywhere in place of commas. The repetition that marks my style. The notebooks and the loose pages bear my mark. They bear my agitation. My confusion. But amongst the notebooks and the loose pages there are other pages. Other pages that assault the notebooks and the loose pages. Other loose pages that do not bear my mark. Do not bear my agitation or confusion. Other pages in different hands, in different inks, in different languages. Pages which contain great errors of grammar. Pages of others. Pages of others, unsigned. Pages which usually open with a cliched phrase: My dear Elias. And pages which do not begin with My dear Elias, but with some other cliched phrase instead: Mr. Elias. Day on day the notebooks and the pages multiply. They stack and swell. They fill the space that is my life. Fill out the blanks. The blanks of my life. The notebooks are new. The pages are new. The notebooks are old and the pages are old. The notebooks and the pages are quite old. They are very old or they are quite old. They are old and torn. So old they're torn. So old the ink is sometimes vanished from the page. No exaggeration: the ink is vanished. The notebooks and the pages are full of the blanks of my life. They start on the shelves and go over the floor. They cover the couches. They climb to the ceiling. My home is an archive. Big archive. Huge archive. The huge archive doesn't bother me. Of course the huge archive doesn't bother me. But what excites my curiosity – what really excites it (excites it to the point of obsession) – is that I know nothing about the archive. As I write now, I do not know a thing about the contents of the archive. Sure, I've looked through the archive. But then again I haven't. I don't know anything about its history. There's a date written in some of the notebooks. Some of the loose pages have dates written on them. But what was I doing on that date? I don't know. I don't remember if I was at all. If I was the protagonist of an event that took place on that date. I was never the protagonist of any event. Never a protagonist on any date. So, I am Elias. I'm not an amnesiac. I repeat: not an amnesiac. I recall my childhood very well. The boyhood years, and adolescence. Myself as a young man, a man grown to maturity, grown old. My death. The funeral. My burial. The streets and alleyways and brothels. These notebooks and loose pages: perhaps they're my stories. My stories at different times. What I'm trying to say is: perhaps I wrote stories at different times. Story-writing's part of who I am now. Has always been, perhaps. Always and forever. Forever and for always. The events in my archive may be in my hand but the events in my archive do not belong to me. No one can say for sure that I'm the same person I was ten years ago. Let us be scientific. All the cells in the stomach are replaced every five years. Red blood cells change every three months. Liver cells in less than a year. The skeleton renews every ten. No cells stay the same except for those in the eye's lens. The cells in the lens and the nerve cells in the brain's meningeal layer. Can I attribute my whole archive to the cells in the lens, to the cells in the meninges? Maybe my archive is simply a history of characters. That I have acted out characters. Have acted them out because I am an actor. A minor actor, but an actor nonetheless. A failed actor. But an actor. As an actor I embody characters. I embody the characters though I am not the characters. The characters are stuck to me. Are stuck to me though I am not them. I utter their speech, though I am not them. I wear their clothes. I watch what they watch. I fuck like they fuck. Maybe, too, I'm killed like they are killed. Without being them. Maybe that is why I witnessed my own funeral. Why I saw the tents erected for my wake. Why I am Elias.

I am Elias, and I live in an archive. In a huge archive. A vast archive. An archive which starts from the balcony. The balcony which looks over the street through a square window. The balcony that links two rooms. The balcony which is full of notebooks and loose pages. The archive covers the bedroom. Covers the whole bedroom, with the exception of the bed. Covers the entrance hall. The whole hall, with the exception of a single chair. It covers the sitting room. There is no furniture in the sitting room. The sitting room is covered by a carpet. Handwoven. High-quality handwoven. The archive reaches the bathroom. The archive breaches the bathroom. Part of the archive waits patiently upon the high shelves. It marches to the kitchen. Pauses by the kitchen door. Proceeds to the office. It fills the office up. I live from corridor to corridor. I live surrounded by a history which belongs to me. By a history which doesn't. Surrounded by a history and knowing nothing of history. To repeat: I know nothing about history. To be clear: maybe it does not belong to me. In this sense, home is like a body. A body, with the body's head the balcony. Its arms the bedroom and the hall. The sitting room its neck. The bathroom is the chest. Kitchen is belly. One leg is the office and the other leg is missing. The body, let's say, is legless. The legless body is like my own. My body, with its missing foot. Conceived this way, my home lacks a male member. But my body doesn't. My body, praise be to God, has a male member. A member I have not lost in this city of losses. A member which has accompanied me through the streets and alleyways and brothels. There is another foot which stands in for my lost one. Another artificial foot. An artificial foot with a special shoe. A foot resembling the original. My artificial foot does not make me feel the loss of the original. But it is different from it. It makes me feel the loss of my original foot. And home is missing a leg. Another leg is with the neighbours. A leg which belongs next door. I am unable to persuade the neighbours to return a room to me. A room to make the body whole. The body of the home. It's no great thing that home be legless. Without a leg, original or artificial. Yet a crisis all the same. A crisis, and no solution to the crisis. In any case, I regard my home's missing leg as amputated. Cut off in a crash. A car crash. A train crash. A crash of the kind that happens in my city every day. City of losses. History, too, is amputated. The leg of history, cut off in a crash. In a car crash, in a train crash, in a crash like the crashes that happen every day in cities like my city. City of losses.

The notebooks and the pages on the shelves. The notebooks and the pages on the floor. And on the wall, the pictures. The pictures cover all the walls. The walls of the bedrooms. The bathroom walls. The kitchen walls. The walls of the sitting room. Pictures that resemble me, and don't. Drawings. Photos in black and white. In colour. Pictures in military uniform. Pictures in the vestment of a priest. A sheikh's robes. School clothes. To be clear: I know nothing about the military. I know nothing about school. I'm not a man of religion. Of any religion. The pictures belong to me, and don't. Pictures of a child. Of a child between a mother and a father. Of the same child between another mother and father. Between a different mother and father. Picture of a man and woman at their wedding celebration. Picture of another man and woman at another wedding celebration. Picture of an old man on a bicycle wearing a beret. Of another old man. A very old man. An old man wearing a robe in the middle of a field. Of a young man with an amputated foot, balanced on a crutch. Of a young man in sunglasses, apparently blind. And other pictures in photo albums. Pictures that resemble me, and don't. Some of the pictures are of people and I don't know any people. I never did. Perhaps I never will.

    Yesterday, I came to this building. I recall that I came to this building. I came here and the day was cold. Very cold. Very — murderously — cold. I don't know why I came to this building. It's not that I don't remember — I do remember — it's just that I don't know why I came to the building. To this building in particular. My clothes were torn. My face was bloodied. My hair in disarray. Disarranged and sticky. Sticky with my blood. Sticky with other blood. I was lately emerged from death. Or had been in confrontation with death. Or had escaped death. I was carrying notebooks under my arm. Notebooks and loose pages. I had fled death with notebooks and loose pages. I entered the building. I knocked on the door of the first apartment. An old woman emerged. A woman, but she resembled me. Old, but she resembled me. She hugged me and said: Elias! Kissed me and said: Elias! Invited me in. Elias! She brought cotton wool and gauze and water and antiseptic. Elias! The woman did not resemble me. The old woman did not resemble me. She was not old, but she was a woman, and she did not resemble me. I was lately escaped from death. I had not come to terms with what had happened to me. Not come to terms with it. The women brought juice and had me drink. She brought food and fed me. I didn't refuse. I didn't object. I didn't say thank you. The woman told me that I had been a quiet child. She told me that I'd been a naughty child. Told me about my mother. Said she'd been my mother's friend. She did not say that my mother had died, but I understood that my mother had died. From the woman's sad expression I understood that my mother had died. From her generous remembrance. From her choice of tenses. We canonise the dead. The dead are always good. The dead guard the living with the spirits of the dead. The woman told me that she had suckled me with this breast. The woman told me she had taught me to read. The woman told me that the woman had told me stories. She said that I used to come and go. That she used to be angry with me. But she was not angry with me. She did not say that my mother was dead. She did not say that my mother had run away. That my mother was gone. The woman told me that the woman had been my mother's friend. Everyone is a friend of the dead. A friend of absent friends. To repeat: everyone is a friend of the dead, a friend of absent friends. Then the woman led me to the bathroom. She brought me a towel. Ran the water warm. Laughed and said: Now shower, Elias. I showered, and as I showered, I thought that the woman's laugh had meant: I won't wash you, Elias! I won't wash you like I used to wash you, Elias. I shan't scrub you like I once did. You're grown, Elias. Look how tall you are, Elias. You're taller than me now, Elias. The shower's jet was drumming on my head. Was falling down and cleansing my head. Was cleansing my head of blood. The shower's jet was falling like bullets. Bullets. And me, lately escaped from bullets. I was going about my business when they opened fire. And I ran away. I had not intended to face the bullets. I'm not such a fool as to face down bullets. I ran from the bullets on my artificial foot. Leglessly. I ran from the bullets, carrying the sound of the bullets with me. The colour of the bullets' victims. The appearance of the gunners. The gunners' black clothes. The gunners' camouflaged clothes. The gunners' white clothes. The appearance of the gunners, with their trimmed beards. The gunners with their long beards. Then I came out of the bathroom. Came out, thinking about the woman. The woman belongs to the same Eliasity, I thought. The same Eliasity, and I am the creator of the Eliasity. Or perhaps only I belong to it. And maybe her name is Elias too. And I put on new clothes. Clean clothes. Clothes untorn. And I sat with the woman. Sat with the woman, aware that she did not resemble me. And though the woman did not resemble me I did not eject her from the Eliasity. The woman gave me a key. She said: The key is the key to my apartment. To your apartment, Elias. She said the apartment was on the third floor. It's on the third floor, Elias. On your left. On your left, Elias. And she went with me when she saw I was confused. She opened the door for me. The woman opened the door for me. Screwed up her face at the dust. I did not screw up my face at the dust, but the woman screwed up hers. She said she would bring me a maid right away. I didn't say no. I didn't object. I didn't refuse. Nor did I consent, though. I shut the door. She invited me to relax in her apartment. My mind wandered. The woman suggested that I do as I pleased. I thought that I was doing as I pleased. But I didn't know what I pleased. She gave me money. I said nothing. I shook my head. I left the apartment not knowing what I pleased. I wandered the streets nearby not knowing what I pleased. The streets nearby were red puddles. Puddles without my pleasing. Red without my pleasing. Red ponds without my pleasing. I went down alleyways to avoid the red puddles and ponds. I saw a red bar. I saw a red coffee shop. I saw a red supermarket. I saw a red traffic light. I saw a red traffic cop. I thought the world must have the measles. The colour red counters measles, I thought. I knew the world did not have measles, but I thought that it must. I don't know why I thought the world must have measles. I saw red men. Red women. Red buildings. Red cars. Red drivers. And I thought the world had measles. From the streets to the alleyways. From the alleyways to the brothels. And the brothels were red. The brothels had measles. But the red of the brothels was different to the red of the streets and alleys. It was different because the measles was different. I believe that the measles was different. I couldn't say why, but the measles was different. And I went back to the building. And in the building I became aware. I became aware that I was wearing red-tinted glasses. The problem was the red glasses. Everything was fine: the problem was that the glasses were red. I was at fault because I'd worn the red glasses. I should wear sea-blue glasses. I should wear field-green glasses. Pink-as-life glasses. I thought I must be in a dream. In a dream in red glasses. I thought I must be in a nightmare. In red glasses in a nightmare. I thought I must be in a game. In a game in red glasses. But I was not in a dream. I was not in a nightmare. I was in no game. I was in Redland. I could see Redland. I did not know what Redland was. But I was there. I opened the door to the apartment and I sat on the ground and I looked at the shelves and I thought I saw red drops dripping from the shelves. Dripping karkadé. Dripping sherbet. Dripping wine. Red wine. The shelves were being pressed. The shelves were serving drinks. I asked the shelves to keep their drinks for now. I asked the shelves to think of tomorrow. And I slept or woke or took off the red glasses, and I looked at the notebooks. Looked at the loose pages. Looked through the loose pages. Read my handwriting. Read my style. Read my signature. But I didn't read anything. I didn't read anything in particular. Just got acquainted with who I was. I was trying to get acquainted with who I was. I looked at the pictures, too. The pictures were plain to see. Quite plain to see. And I wandered through the apartment. Became aware that the apartment was legless. The one-legged apartment. It was at this moment I became aware that the apartment resembled me. That the body of the apartment resembled my body. I felt the tragedy of having an artificial foot. I felt the blessing that it was not amputated.

Now, I wander through the apartment. I wander one-legged through the apartment. I wander through it like a ghost. Like a ghost I wander, and I do not know the ghost. I do not know the ghost's past. The ghost's history. A ghost searching through loose pages for the ghost it is. Through loose pages. Through lined notebooks. Notebooks made up of many pages. Through pages inscribed in the ghost's hand. Through pages inscribed in others' hands: the hands of other ghosts. In the hand of a ghost who is also writing other pages. Who is publishing stories in newspapers in return for pay. Who is working as an actor. Who knows that he is a failed writer of stories. Who is searching through the ghost's stories for the same ghost. Who is searching for the character of the same ghost in the ghost's films. Who is hanging the stories on the wall of the ghost's home. Who is avoiding the pronouns. Stories next to pictures. A present next to a past. A present next to a past of others. A past of others next to the ghost's past. The ghost's past and the ghost's present next to the ghost's future. The ghost's good leg next to the ghost's lame leg. The ghost's original leg next to the ghost's artificial. And as I wander, I think of ordering the chaos. Numbering the notebooks' pages. Numbering the loose pages. Numbering is sequence. Sequence produces order. Order leads to something. Something useful. Usually something useful. The useful is usually something. But I don't like order. Order is routine. Order is boring. Order leads to sequence. Sequence leads to expectation. Expectation's bad. And I am Elias. Despite it all, I am Elias.

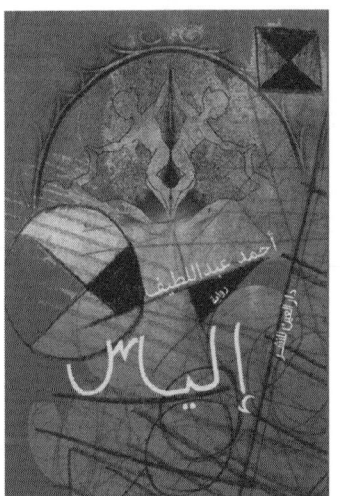

Elias, published by Dar Al-Ain, Cairo 2014

SAMER ABU HAWWASH

That isn't the way to make pizza

AND OTHER POEMS

TRANSLATED BY RAPHAEL COHEN

DIYAA'S POEM

Pain, you say . . .
"Pain that would take three lifetimes to heal."
I stand alone in front of a lone mirror
repeating your name
whispering your name
cursing your name
so my heart learns to listen
so it doesn't try to correct me
breathless my entire life
cursing your entire life
weeping for your eyes
your mouth, your laugh
your breasts
the daylight of your soul
the way that you listen to music
that you rub creams on your body
that you wash your hair
that you type on the computer
that you get ready to go to sleep
that you say my name

without me this time
and without my spouting nonsense too.

SAMER ABU HAWWASH

Is life more beautiful now . . . without that pain?
"Pain that would take three lifetimes to heal."
Have you become more wonderful, confident, calm, secure
without that man with a beer belly
who makes little effort to get rid of it
smokes a cigarette factory every night
glugs a brewery every night
and then complains of something in his chest
or his heart
and natters about his fear of cancer
before snoring like a locomotive in bed!

At least now you don't have to deal with all that:
with the television that expanded over the years
till it filled the wall
with the worn-out old sofa
that I still cherished
with the films you had to watch
as if you were in a temple
with my constant talk about death
and my constant silence about death . . .

You no longer have to put up with my nightmares before sleep
or drive away my demons after.

If not that
then at least
you no longer have to remind me constantly
to lift the toilet seat
and close the shower curtain
or set an alarm
for when to take the pill
or leave tampons once a month
somewhere obvious in the bathroom

At least now you can eat spaghetti
lasagne and sushi
and other foods I deprived you of . . .
But tell me,

you whose intuition I often trusted
even when it was wrong,
has your intuition told you lately how much I loved you – do love
   you?
Do you understand the
   extent/depth/distance/time/space/possibilities/pain with
   which I loved you – do love you?

Do you sense that in my hands now
is only a handful of air
saying your name
and your name alone?

Are you listening to a lot of sad music these days?
Jazz . . .
Dalida . . .
Ella Fitzgerald . . .
Edith Piaf perhaps . . .
but definitely not Fairouz.

Do you remember our last trip
the way you stopped a man to ask the way to the hotel:
"Bonjour, monsieur . . ."
as though accusing him of a crime . . .
and all the laughter that followed?

(Isn't that what love is
Lots of laughter
and few reasons?)

That laughter in bed
that jumping into bed.

Long discussions about sex
long talks about love.

Can a man love two women at the same time?
I don't know. I don't think so.
Can you love two women at the same time?

SAMER ABU HAWWASH

I know that I loved you two, three, a hundred times.
You were/you are all my secret lovers . . .

Now I think I know that pain
The pain from your not having loved a woman like you
so you would know what it means
for a man like me to love a woman like you

and no longer be able to/willing to
look for any woman but her?

Now it's this pain
"Pain that would take three lifetimes to heal" . . .
So listen to French songs
turn off your phone
get rid of the pack of contraceptives
put all the photos in drawers
drink a glass of wine
scream out your pain in front of the screen
take half a sleeping pill
go to sleep

and don't forget to shut the curtains

in my face.

WE WILL BE SAVED

We'll come off the motorway of love
we'll curse the engineers of the road and the heart
we'll quarrel a little because we missed the exit
we'll get lost in desolate cities
improvised in the heat by a scintillating vision
we'll search in the desert for our house
for our names
on dusty signposts
we'll regret a lost afternoon;

in sorrow
we'll ask the ghosts of the highway
the way
to the way.
We'll fill lost time with dismay
and true to the situation
we'll exchange jazz for a tawdry love song
sung by a Lebanese in an Egyptian accent;
we'll read life's palm in the sand
and in the heights
a plastic clown laughs at us
and we will never discover anything we didn't know before
but in the end we will be saved
because – if we recognize we are totally lost –
our eyes will show us ourselves
and we will know that our hands
that have said nothing till now
remember the way better than us.

MAKING UP

Love, I think I should get you back together with yourself
buy you a motorbike
invite you to the seaside
where we can sit down at an abandoned café
and contemplate the ordinary wave
washing the feet of passersby with its eyes
as it secretly ebbs away.
Then you'll need no more than a sigh
to forgive the slips of your soul
no more than a glance
to fill the pockets of your desolate children
with
  stars.

SAMER ABU HAWWASH

THAT ISN'T THE WAY TO MAKE PIZZA

What matters is the dough
then add whatever toppings you like,
said one of us all of a sudden
I don't remember who now,
perhaps we had heard it on a cookery programme
or from a friend
or maybe we shouted it out together
in a moment of total despair.

In front of an unfortunate grey lump
I stand stunned, nonplussed, stupid
like a soldier who's failed to carry out orders.
You come into the kitchen
give one look at the dough
and sigh, "Tut, tut.
That isn't the way to make pizza."
Then you go out laughing.

I try to fix it
I add a dash of water
a dash of flour
a dash of hope.
I try again
but as usual
my prayers let me down
and my swearing gives me away.

I hear a voice speaking to me from the ceiling
or maybe from my life history:
"Man,
hasn't anyone ever told you:
'That isn't the way to make pizza'?"

Dear God,
at this time
in this life

SAMER ABU HAWWASH

I'm not asking you for
more than one base
in the shape of a circle.

You come into the kitchen
look with pity at the dough
now shaped like a dying animal.
You look at my hands
then my face
trying to stifle your laugher.

"I know . . . That isn't the way to make pizza,"
I tell you,
trying to stifle my tears.
Finally,
I throw the dough in the bin
and leave the kitchen.

At night in bed
in the pale light
coming from the balcony,
terrified, I look deep into your eyes.
Apologetically, you look deep into mine
and sigh
as if to say:
"Never mind,
we'll try again next time."

I sigh
as if to say:
"Only if
you don't give up
so fast."

But, my darling,
what if there isn't
another time?

SAMER ABU HAWWASH

SMALL PLANS

Don't decide to stop smoking. Make an alternative, more realistic plan. Say you're going to smoke a cigarette every hour and set the alarm of your mobile to ring at the set time, as if by its own willpower. Then reward yourself by waiting for the next cigarette.

Don't decided to stop quarrelling with your partner for good. You know that promises are like a German film pirated in China with the subtitles for another film or that stops working in the middle of the action. So be content to tell your partner that you won't quarrel for a whole week, from Tuesday to Tuesday for instance.

Don't decide to erase your bad memories all in one go. To absent friends in particular devote three minutes before bed, two minutes asleep, and one minute on waking. Don't allow any of them to take up more time or enter the dream of another absent friend.

Like buying a house in instalments, you divide up the pain you've experienced into instalments. You try to overlook what you don't know like you would a neighbour you deliberately postpone getting to know.

Or like a cigarette you tuck behind your ear in the knowledge that the mobile will ring at the expected time by its very own willpower.

BREEZE

This breeze is my father's hands
smoothing down my hair.
This fog
is his gaze
over the night of my life.
This cloud
is his thought of the
remaining daylight
in the shade of the porch.

SAMER ABU HAWWASH

A SMALL GOD BURSTS INTO TEARS

Another small god
bursts into tears
on my shoulder
for an obscure reason
or a crystal-clear reason
and for the same reason
I name him the night that has now ended
the night that has passed
or the moment that passed a moment ago
like a stain, wiped from the table
by a blind waitress.

AFTER ZIAD RAHBANI

So die the dry tear below the eye and the raindrop suspended below the window. The neighbour's dog dies, and the doormat and the doorbell. Even the door dies. The transient joy of a dying man dies too, and the man's voice, and the man's laugh, and his height. New shoes, the fast road and the slow road, the shade of the sleeping tree, the shade of the house, and the ghosts of the house die. Grandmother's bed dies and grandmother's chair and grandmother's fig tree. Even grandmother dies. Hands that love and that kill and that run and that toil and that grind rock and knead trees, and that sing and dream and when they remember, regret, and when they forget, regret, all die. The cat on the doorstep, the clock on the wall, the scent of the cupboard, the day off on Sunday, new clothes for Eid, the sight of the sea, even the waves of the sea, die. Anguish of heart, a stammer of longing, a bleat of pain, paroxysms of joy, these too die.

This long summer that we thought shone in the heart, burns first then dies.

SAMER ABU HAWWASH

AFTER BOB DYLAN

I watched a man drag a house, who said he wanted to put it by the sea, and a beautiful lame woman drag a nation of lame children behind her. Words barking and sundry levels of silence dragged by horses. I watched black plastic bags blow across the desert and a long-haired blonde flash her breasts at God and cry. I watched a friend who died in his sleep smile through the rain. I watched the rain too. I watched trains smash into bedrooms, and flashing mirrors shattered by looks. And looks that shattered themselves. A boy in shorts jumped to touch a butterfly he thought was a cloud. Old black people practised rap through teeth clenched in anger. Philosophers tried in vain to interpret a coconut. I watched clay pitch a tent and mud dig secret trenches. I watched the sixties approach me with outstretched arms and two black crows caw on their shoulders. I watched naked happiness skip. I watched my grandmother swim in a glass. I watched my father growing on a wall. I watched the nineties as a paper plane dissolve in the mist.

THE WEATHER'S LOVELY IN BEIRUT

I can hardly breathe. I'm not responsible for Baghdad. It's not me who made Saddam so stupid or who whispered, high on heroin, in Bush's ears. I can hardly hear the sound of the air-conditioner, or canary song, or the crow of the neighbour's cockerel at five in the afternoon and which I've started thinking seriously about slaughtering. I'm not responsible for Palestine. I didn't tell Hitler to kill a hundred billion Jews and I didn't tell my grandfather to leave Haifa and walk to Beirut. I can hardly pick up my legs and take a step; I sometimes forget the right order and take two successive steps with my right leg. When someone asks me about the situation in Lebanon, I feel I'm standing on top of a skyscraper in Dubai with vertigo. Then after a while I add: "But the weather's lovely in Beirut . . ." Yes, that's definite. The weather's lovely in Beirut.

From his collection *Laysa Hakatha Tusna'a Alpizza*
(That isn't the way to make pizza)
published by Al-Mutawassit, Milan, Italy, 2016

Travels

Farouk Yousif, New York
Hassouna Mosbahi, Andalusia
Abdelkader Benali, Tangier
Monir Almajid, Matsuyama
Saïd Khatibi, Sarajevo

FAROUK YOUSIF

A Poet in New York
In the Footsteps of Federico García Lorca

TRANSLATED BY CHIP ROSSETTI

> You run, afraid of arriving too late
> After heaven's door is closed,
> And you come across the sign in bold type:
> It's Not Here.
> So you sit and wait
> And hear from all sides
> No, It's Not Here.
> And you say to everyone around you
> No, It's Not Here.
> And they sit and wait.
> And you sit and wait.
>
> *Tawfiq Sayegh, "Poem K"*

Imperfect Keys to Invisible Doors

The City

New York most resembles a book you can start reading on any page you wish. Just set foot on the sidewalk and walk. The city is all around you. It is all those visible and hidden neighborhoods after you lose your desire to see everything. Your first outing can persuade you to put off that desire until further notice. The place robs you of the ability to grasp it once you've succumbed to its visual assault and are satisfied with thumbnail images of it.

Farouk Yousif

There is a strong wind that carries everything along with it but your eye can only see a rhythm, which indicates that the city is still there, but on its flight of stairs is music. You lift your head but have no control over the movement of your body, which turns in a circle, compelled to dance. Nothing in New York can be seen as it is. It is enough for you to see what you love in it and through it, if you are fortunate enough to stumble upon its transparent parts. For it is solid, silent marble. Thick, dark glass. A city wicked in its love for and obsession with its beauty. If you love it recklessly, then that's no reason to hope it will love you back. New York is a complete city. What does it mean that there is a complete city there? There is the tree and a person's attempt to search within it for a defect that will lead to its autumn losses. Nature will laugh. You will have to think of a way to deal with a planet that was created in secret in order to stir the senses with its nervous disorder. You can't be calm when faced with a single square meter of that city. There are angels that laugh as they sit quietly on the corners of that square meter. Square meters, each one of them pointing to another. You can't stumble on the imperfect part amid all that perfection. You can look for the beaver's dam beneath the Brooklyn Bridge, but you won't find it. New York can be viewed from above as a maze. An imagined geometry that flows out to infinity. As for the New York in whose streets you walk, it's a city that invents its images at every glance. It takes form only to be something else.

> NewNewNew
> YoYoYo
> rkrkrk

The Titanic and the Stock Exchange and Rashid Hussein and Rockefeller Center and the Empire State Building and Walt Whitman and the UN Security Council and the Statue of Liberty and the island of Manhattan and MoMA and the Brooklyn Bridge and Broadway theaters and Henri Michaux and Jackson Pollock and Union Square and Harlem and Frank Sinatra and Whitney Houston and the Hudson River and Barry White. Nothing of New York is present without a mask. A city of masks that tell lies for the sake of fashioning their truths. New York is a miracle. The language of extinct family trees opens up onto joyous surprises. It is a flower made of stone, and a stone lighter than a bubble.

> It is a grave
> It is a park
> And it is a skyscraper

It is 748 square kilometers, the area of the modern Noah's Ark.

It is five boroughs, zones for suffering language loss. Brooklyn, Queens, Manhattan, The Bronx, Staten Island. A Tower of Babel where the inhabitants speak hundreds of languages.

New York is a capital of finance, arts, education, fashion, and diplomacy. The city where the largest number of foreigners in the world live.

FAROUK YOUSIF

The People

Americans are real people just like us. Tormented and miserable, estranged and lost, although it's easy to join them in mocking the barbarity of endless space. A throng of humanity filled with health and strength. Athletes promote a nutritional diet in opposition to fast food. There are a lot of nature conservation lands for running and walking everywhere. When you're in a hurry, you get a greater share of conspicuous sympathy. When you stand there, in confusion, looking for the right exit in a subway station, often a man or woman will surprise you with an offer of assistance. Something like that happens all the time, and the city is swarming with foreigners who don't carry maps, like me. They are a people at peace with itself, who understand that geography is a complex question, one that lends itself to being a subject of conversation between strangers. There is a kind of mental collapse that maps can't help with. The similarity of names is enough to paralyze all the senses. New York won't give you the chance to distinguish between two streets that share the same name. So you sometimes have to play the role of a blind person and let others take the lead. On my way to the Whitney Museum I stopped an elegantly dressed man carrying a briefcase, looking as if he were the head of a law firm, and I asked him for directions. All he did was take out his phone and start looking for the shortest way to get me to the museum. This is a city unlike other cities. People there orient themselves to what you ask of them. There are always strangers on the street and it's up to you to help them, turning to modern technologies for assistance. People in New York are stepladders, except they all offer a speedy response and look upon you as a stranger who merits assistance. But if you come across a homeless person, you won't ask him. The homeless, who are innumerable, are spread out far from the center of Manhattan. They take refuge in a tragic silence. New York has the greatest number of homeless you can see in one city. And if you don't count it as a city, it's a free-for-all planet. You can imagine Manhattan's clientele as astronauts. Each one is looking in a direction that interests him, after landing there in order to do just that. There is no center. I mean the shared language. This is a planet of languages, all of them speaking in English.

You think about poverty's senses
About its sleeping sentinels
And you ask, "Does poverty have no doors?"
Wealth yawns
There are dogs with open mouths but no bark,
They are merely puppets
The gardens of the rich evoke a memory of the Great Gatsby

Time

We know more about time than time knows about itself. Those are small wars that take place like an explosion on a shore inhabited by naked men coming out of temples, with beads that surround their necks with cryptic prayers. In that city that is fearful of time, words don't sit on lines, nor do lines crouch beneath words. Time leaps like a beautiful word among the strings of a violin in the hands of a girl who just emerged from the subway, out of breath. At the end of the street stand muggers with guns. Right away, the muggers are afraid of the music and the girl walks quickly past them. Before their hands can reach for their guns, the girl disappears, leaving no trace of herself except her scent. All the clocks on the street and on buildings are working, but show different times. The time of cotton, wood, paper, spices, and freed slaves. But what time is it? I thought of Tawfiq Sayegh, who kept his watch synchronized to Beirut's time. Five hours' difference separated me from the time in London, where I reside.

I sit by the riverside so I can describe what I see. In front of me is Manhattan. Red buildings that look alike. I am in Brooklyn. Water passes by like time. I was thinking about what was happening in Silicon Valley and on Shaykh 'Umar Street at the same time. I look at my shadow. A sunny day in a land where the sun shows up late. On my way to the river I saw a French café. "I'll go there on my way back. It's still early," as if time were a cat holding off meowing until the sparrow shakes the tree branch with its feet. The sight of Manhattan at a distance can open the door to a waking trance. A person can see everything in order to fall asleep. He can remember his childhood and youth in order to forget. A soft machine that runs with a marvelous smoothness. There are those who are waiting for the ap-

Federico García Lorca

pearance of the carpet on the other side. Hundreds of Iranians spend their time weaving that carpet carrying the image of the Great Satan. The ghost of that joke never leaves me. I think about those who call for "Death to America" without having seen a single stone of New York. Sufi excesses can be a subject for satirical cartoon magazines. Time here resembles a fast-moving wheel, whether you possess the ability to roll with it—something unheard-of—or whether you stand there watching contemplatively on the sidewalk. Time is solid: it causes injuries and doesn't slip through your fingers the way it does when it's liquid. When I went back to the French café, I was transported to another era. Edith Piaf was singing. The waitress came up to me and spoke to me in French, so I smiled at her out of love. I didn't tell her I was there. There, like a cloud, I had no time and no language.

I am Harun al-Rashid's clock going to Charlemagne

I am Big Ben and the gleam of the diamond on the wrist of a sullen princess

There is a Chinese man counting grains of sand falling like tears from my eye

FAROUK YOUSIF

The Subway

The subway map makes it easy for visitors to use the fastest means of getting around, but the capacity of many of the main stations in New York frustrate that optimism. Moving from one line to another requires you to leave the station only to enter it somewhere else, which can sometimes be far from the place you came out of. I have lost a lot of time looking for the entrance to the stairs leading to the train line I wanted to get on. On the way, you stumble upon a lot of stories that took place and left traces that are still evident. The thief that got to the meaning before you did and took it for himself, leaving nothing for you except empty shapes. Just squares on the ground that feet have walked on for dozens of years. The day itself hasn't passed by. It's the people that changed. It won't do you any good to walk slowly. In a heroic frenzy, you will rush to come in first in the race where the starting whistles were blown somewhere far off. And because the subway stations in New York are empty except for the few escalators whose steps you can't count as you go up. Half the effort you make is spent going up and down, but the other half is spent trying to get on the train first so you can get an empty seat. There are trains marked with letters and others with numbers, and there are stations that have more than one name. There are stations that are practically labyrinths; compared to them, the Gare St. Lazare in Paris is child's play. Corridors that don't take you where you want to go, and others that open up onto corridors that branch out into still others. Every time you try to exit, there is something that drives you to despair.

472 stations.

And one traveler.

He's that poet who is asking his shadow not to follow him.

The Poet

Federico García Lorca beat me here by ninety years. He was thirty years old, an owl that alighted there between the years 1929 and 1930. Six years later, Franco's forces would execute him in a village in southern Spain.

"I knew they had killed me.
They searched for me in cafés, graveyards, and churches
They opened barrels and cabinets
They stole three skeletons
To pull out their gold teeth
But they didn't find me."

    I had decided to follow in his footsteps without being optimistic that I would find a trace of him. In this city that disowns itself at every moment, it's impossible to stumble upon a glass of wine that Lorca left behind, full to overflowing, in a bar on Broadway, after a friend invited him to talk in private in an alley nearby. I read his book of verse, *A Poet in New York*, on the plane several times. It's a book that can be read from every angle. It can be read from right and left, from above and below. You can start from any line and it will bump up against you. Lorca was looking for Spain in New York, but he couldn't find it. At the time, New York wasn't the global city it became after the Second World War. But it wasn't possible for a European poet dreaming of nature. I read Lorca and sometimes feel pity for him. He saw another city, other than the one whose rhythmic footsteps he listened to on its sidewalks. I follow him and see what his eyes didn't fall upon. "He beat me to the whispers that I won't be able to hear," I tell myself as I walk along, banishing from my sight his night of despair. Stupid Manhattan is happy with its strength, its money, and its power. Its light teases the eyelashes of those sleeping on the other shores of the Atlantic. Before the statue of Simon Bolivar, the liberator of Latin America, I stood and thought about Lorca. "Possibly his night was diminished here." His ghost had left the book to accompany me, but many times it didn't know the way. I close my eyes on his words and see him with his eyes closed, blinded by the lights of the city that he didn't see, ninety years before the eyes of the man that followed in his footsteps.

Like the gypsies, I waited for you
And I danced for your arrival
And like the gypsies, I wept
Because your shadow motioned to me like a stranger
It passed me by and didn't talk to me
It left me all alone.

FAROUK YOUSIF

Manhattan, Soft in the Head
A Butterfly that Drowned in the Inkwell

I am a bird. I arrive as a bird. The sea there is below me. The sea is not the only thing below me. There are stories that were never told about ships that didn't arrive, ships that are still on the way, and ships that are not yet built. There weren't ferries for the dead in those days. The boats were made of wood. Boats didn't go too far from shore. There was a safety rope tied in a way that made it possible for someone to feel confident about his family sitting and waiting for him at the dinner table. A single candle for reading. There is a man reading and a woman amusing herself by looking out the window. The woman sitting beside me is blond and speaks Arabic, which she had learned in one intensive year of living in Damascus. "*Ya Mustafa, Ya Mustafa*," she sings, as if she were waiting for me to start clapping out in nostalgia for Syria, so she could dance before the plane took off. In the field were two swallows, three calves, and a horse. Without ink, I write. I dream of a lake of ink that cannot be seen but rather smelled like the scent of Aleppo's olive-oil soap. I dream of flowers blossoming out of the sand. Outside the plane the clouds look like bags stuffed with white cotton. Resin flows on the tree trunk. Fingers there sketch faces that imitate their masks. It isn't a storm. It's the laughter of a woman giving in to the past. I focus my eyes to read. There is a book that is still open. When books are closed, birds lose their wings. The dream will be warm like the imprint of a head on a pillow. It isn't night. It's a well with steps of silk. I glide quietly to that well. Whoever has reached its darkness ahead of me can see me. It has my face—it was reflected in its water.

"You are the mirror of my pain," it laughs. "So you are the one I killed," it weeps. "What happened," he says, "can take place at any moment when the butterfly drowns in an inkwell. Let the ink be blue and let the kitchen in your house, there in the distant capital city, be its star. And let the butterfly press its wings to its windowpane and die."

The butterfly isn't New York. It's a visitor who has been killed.

The prophecy of the child with the round white face should not have landed in the fruit bowl. I will not believe that the hand of

heaven kills. The woman sitting beside me informs me that living in New York brings a person close to heaven.

"I am a bird," she tells me. I turn to look at her. I see her differently. She didn't want to dance to the tune of an old song. She was another woman. A British woman who works in New York. My daughter works there as well. "On Wall Street?" "No, at a foundation for the arts." Arabs are good at investing money. And they are lost, too. She is silent. The butterfly isn't alone in the darkness of the ink. There are poets and union workers and agitators and gangsters and murder victims and recluses and spreaders of rumors and makers of painted miniatures and barefoot musicians and night-time artists and smokers and those saved from danger and storytellers of a rebellious nature and chic beggars and imams without tombs and rebels whose feet have been taken by the water, leaving them on the shore.

From London to New York you will lose five hours. Around ninety years ago, Lorca lost days. Afterward, he lost his life. My Granada is Granada. New York inspired a moment of escape in his life. The blue that dreams and the blue that must be and the blue that is a sole possibility.

I will sit on the banks of the Hudson and weep. In the field there is still room for two swallows and three calves and a single horse. Ever since I realized that poetry isn't useful, but it is necessary, I talk to the grass as if it were capable of language before language gradually drives its meanings down the path of madness. The waters of the river have swallowed up a lot of sighs. I am building you a bridge of sighs so that we can cross over it together to an island where no one will hurt us. Oh my friend, you who learned from Lorca a way of looking at flowers, you can still wait for me so together we can walk the meter the murdered poet didn't reach.

I am like you
A victim, although I, like you, play the role of the killer
So that others can't see my humiliation
I am broken like a word that no one has uttered
I am lost like a tear that no eye shed
I am stray like a song that is hard to play on the violin.

October 3, 2017, on the Norwegian plane

I Fall Like an Apple

Night is there. It embraces the city whose windows look out over the world and whose doors are shut to loan sharks and bankers and bons vivants of art and elevator manufacturers and game designers and barefoot dancers and those who skate on the quicksilver of mirrors, the images of which show the effect of lashings from the storm, of those putting together sentences out of thin air, and of elegant murderers. Nothing is devoid of elegance in a place that can't be described. It is neither wide nor cramped. I am not alone in that place but my isolation is as confining as a sleeping bag. I should have stayed asleep until the next day's sun beat on my door. It's a sun that was five hours late. Aren't I a piece of paper? I look at my open book and think about open doors in cities I have visited in the past. A friend's laughter shakes loose a bunch of grapes borrowed from the Baroque Period. "I will give you my shoes so that your feet can dream my dreams," an international friend says to me. He kept his window open overlooking Granada because Lorca recommended that. The driver isn't thinking about his shoes, but through them. My friend laughs because the cup overflowed and only Rembrandt's Night Watch was left on the street. "You will run, but you won't reach" that genuine friend. "Put your apple on the table and follow me," he said. "But I am the apple that had fallen from the loftiest heights." I look at Manhattan. An opportunity to see it from above. I know that I will always be below. I read *Alice in Wonderland* several times and it inspired me with the different sizes I later got to know in the maze. Rabbit, I will follow you to strange lands where poetry will be the chirping of morning sparrows. In blue work clothes I will find my star and go with it to the movie theater. He will be called a rich man in disguise. That is true, but I am coming as a poet walking in the footsteps of a poet who went before me. Ninety years ago, Lorca preceded me to America. There was another America. But America is America. Opulence and hardship. Wealth and poverty. Aggression and camaraderie. Generosity and theft. Lorca will not be waiting for me at JFK Airport. I will arrive, sleeping, just as the poet arrived, the poet who is now placing his cheek on the damp grass, dreaming of the night of his murder. "What's with the necktie?" the flight attendant says when I ask her why daylight is traveling with us. Daylight outside the plane and night-time within. I smiled because of the five hours added to my life. What can a person do in those five hours? Fall like an apple that is drawn in order to regain its life in art. Draw a line between the bell and its eye-pounding ringing. A relationship evoking the one between a foot and a step that leaves a print on the grass. Rural people with sharpened senses. No ant could stick his nose out without feeling danger. Because a poet is a wild creature, and danger attracts him, he is surrounded by his senses on all sides. Poetry is a dangerous occupation. So is travel. There are those who travel in order to be a stranger. "You'll be a stranger like me," the poet laughs. "But I carry maps that will show me the way to follow you." "You won't find me because my maps that you are carrying with you have been torn by the streets and roads that made a miracle of a city that doesn't belong to our world. Forget Europe and Asia and begin your morning with New York's sun."

O shore where the Atlantic ends
O shore bringing forth desolation from the ground like a grave

O shore drowning in light

Isn't the murdered poet still sitting in one of your bars as he counts his fingers looking for a lost bull and a matador pinned to his horse, waiting for the roar of the crowd?

October 3, 2017 on board the plane and at JFK Airport

As Though It's Manhattan

A person resides in a ground-floor apartment in Brooklyn and that is a surprise that no one expects. This isn't New York. It's as if I alighted on a house with a cement garden that is located next to a church. On the road from JFK Airport, the gleam of Manhattan came from far off to the right. A column of fire marked out the Empire State Building. "Is that always there?" The view was different for Lorca coming by ship. I will put off looking for the hidden streets that Henry Miller walked. From Meserole Avenue where I live to Franklin Street, ten minutes away. From there you can see Manhattan, but from behind a fence. I had to look for a street leading to the river's edge. All Miller did was raise his voice with insults and be hit with frustration when he saw those gloomy buildings that blocked the way. I didn't feel hopeless. The blue is there, while Manhattan is as far from Mexico as it is from me.

Yesterday evening in a Mexican restaurant, a loud conversation was taking place in Spanish. Who was talking to whom? When I discovered that the person who had brought water to our table was also a customer, I understood part of the riddle that question addressed. You don't need to talk to yourself when you are loudly raving, since no one is following every word you're saying. It's not easy to be Mexican. Here everyone was Mexican, with the same height and the same features. And there was the head chef who looked like Hugo Chavez. He was the most Mexican of them all, laughing in a way that revealed the happiness of the moment, when the angels stop recording people's actions. You need to meet a Mexican to forget New York. I remembered there was someone who said: "Poor Mexico! So far from God, so close to the United States!"

That kind of solution won't be useful on Seventh Avenue in Manhattan. It's the street that has entirely become Times Square. The rule of amusement spread forth its monsters. A monster in every alleyway and a puppet that ridicules itself and others. There is no island that welcomes its visitors the way Manhattan does. Perhaps we should have thought about its freedom, not ours. There is violence on the sidewalk. Soft and clean, but its elegance is nearly injured.

It isn't stones. Talk is heavier than stones.

Manhattan, soft in the head.

Its visitors grow more charming when they lose their minds in order to stay balanced. There are those who smile at you as if promising they'll keep a shared secret. A gathering of madmen. I promise you a day that resembles my night so you can visit me carrying your sun like an umbrella.

I am your companion; did I lose the way in the forest?

On Seventh Avenue the forest seems like a forest, but it isn't.

The city lies, but no one saw it.

A girl, naked but for a trace of underwear on her body, comes up to me. Not a bit of snickering, as if we were at a funeral. Passersby don't turn to look at us and no one feels embarrassed. "Do you want to take a picture with me?"

Smiling, I shake my head no and she moves away, showing no expression at all on her face. The neon signs around us strike our hearts before they strike our eyes, and the only thing you can do is walk past them like the others do. The only thing you can do is walk past. Sound and image. Head and foot. Deed and thought. There is a savagery that solidifies its hopelessness through an incongruent opulence and there is an alphabet of images that created its myth on a heap of languages.

On that street you will be one of a thousand. One of a million.

As soon you turn your back, you lose your place. There are those who dream of vanishing before you.

It isn't Manhattan, then. It seemed like it to me. As if it were Manhattan. The piano keys won't pose questions to the playing fingers after the playing has stopped.

"I wanted to talk to you about lost humans."

"What I want to talk to you about is lost dreams."

"That's the difference between us. Manhattan is a dream demolished by lost humans."

October 4, 2017, Times Square

FAROUK YOUSIF

A Moon That No One Understands

Either it was like the zero in a calculation error, which is an emotional question, or it was tempting me to go out naked in the rain, which is an athletic question.

Zero isn't always itself, but it only brought out of its coat two luxuriant breasts as though the rain had entrusted them with its secret.

There, Lorca's "moon that no one understands" doesn't joke around.

It isn't zero and it isn't a cloud. There is a woman that promises you something you won't understand. I imagined that Lorca himself, the Arab Lorca, was sitting on a polished stone bench, without putting his hand to his pocket to take out papers on which he had written his elegy to himself, "If I die, leave the balcony open."

"Not a single balcony is opened in Manhattan."

I will tell you the tale according to the holy books: "There were two girls who wanted to draw water from the well. When the Prophet saw them he offered to help them get water and one of them felt desire for him. When their aged father learned of this, he offered to marry off his daughter to him."

If the events of that tale had taken place in New York, an amusement park would have been built for it.

New York is also a holy city, but of a different kind.

The naked girl I saw in Times Square is a Babylonian priestess.

Maybe no one in New York thinks about the moon. It's a rustic superstition that brings us back to Baghdad. The moon in Granada was something else. The Arabs will only understand the moon of Ibn Zurayq of Baghdad. "In Baghdad God set down a moon for me / In the district of Karkh, it orbits my heart." And because Ibn Zurayq didn't substitute his night for day, he was asleep when the angels were present. But Lorca looked with questioning eyes at the angels when he was murdered.

You shouldn't think about Walt Whitman. New York isn't America. It's a city that commemorates Christopher Columbus's conquest of lands whose original inhabitants have become merely ghosts: you can meet one of them without being obliged to stand out of respect for him. For he is a refugee. It isn't bad for someone to be a refugee, provided that that misfortune doesn't befall him on his own land.

"I will talk to you about the marginalized. My father was one, and he passed that quality down to me," said my landlady. Her father had fled to the United States with the first wave of refugees coming from Europe after the rise of the Nazis. When André Breton came, he went to welcome him, as if he were preparing to meet a king. He was also a surrealist poet. "Don't you like surrealism?" she asked in a serious way. "I haven't given the subject much thought, but I have a great respect for Breton personally." When her father worked in investment in the real estate sector, he forgot about poetry, but he stayed loyal to his marginality. He was a refugee until the day he died, and he didn't advertise his Americanness. He was an old Pole.

"It wasn't because he was Jewish. But because he was a poet."

At the MoMA PS1 Museum this morning, I saw an exhibit about a life that was only lived metaphorically.

Did You Live So You Could Be Struck by the Moment of Your Death?

"It isn't necessary for you to have lived that life for it to invite you into it metaphorically." That is what the docent told you at the MoMA PS1 museum, but it's a shocking and frightening idea. There is an individual undertaking the job of docent who stands between a person and his senses. But what is that inscrutable individual doing in his job? The experience I have lived through wasn't something I made up. You can't see an exhibit by yourself. That's not hypothetical – it's a fact. One of the young people gathered us together to make up a tour group and walked ahead of us towards where we were heading. But where we were heading was imaginary from my point of view, which perhaps was not correct. In his reality, that exhibit didn't include anything that could be seen with your own eyes, such that you could go directly up to it. In order to see, you need someone to guide you to the artworks. There is a hole in the ground, two centimeters in diameter, for example, through which a short video is shown, consisting of a woman saying a sentence you won't be forced to hear. The information reaches you without your feeling the need to know the details. Shabby walls harmonizing with the concept of the exhibit in praise of fragility. You stand in front of the artwork but you don't see it. It's a part of the place. However, the site wasn't suitable in its current role as a place for exhibiting works of art. There was no division between the site and the works of art that we had been guided to by the docent, who was essentially a tape recorder. The young man had been instructed on what to say inasmuch as he was smiling stupidly, without getting rattled when a question was asked of him. But I saw a work by Sol LeWitt among those inscrutable works of art: it was something shocking, in my opinion. But wait. LeWitt established his fame on the basis of his marginalization. He was always abundantly American. I had wandered among the eight floors of the Whitney Museum but didn't happen upon any artistic heights. You can feel happiness because you've seen it. Who is this "Edward Hopper" whom Americans consider a symbol of their artistic purity? A single centimeter of Willem de Kooning, the Dutch artist who became American, is better than all of Hopper's works.

The problem is that no one believes that America is a culturally fragile country. What it really is is a continent. A continent relaxing with what it believes is fitting for itself and what will be acceptable to the world. Didn't it mock us with the Pop Art it borrowed from the UK? Didn't it make us believe that Andy Warhol was an artist of the highest caliber, when he was the one who sang the praises of garbage and filled museums with it? You feel pain when you see important sites dedicated to what you believe is a kind of childish game. This part of the Museum of Modern Art, in one of the world's biggest art-promoting cities, can't be a stage for emptiness. I walked with the others behind that docent, but didn't see a single work of art. There were just damaged walls that you could find anywhere. It wasn't appropriate then for me to express the truth of my feelings, which is what always happens, making it seem more like I was perjuring myself. A lie should remain blossoming in the open. It's an art capital and unfortunately a machine for lying at the same time. I stupidly started off my days there.

5 October 2017

In the park along the East River, on the Brooklyn side, in the morning

1.
The park isn't its plants, but rather the spirits that inhabit it
There a flower shyly smiles whenever it sees me pass by

2.
The chirping that lives in the tree is the call of the mother of sunset
The scent of lost children flows along the fences

3.
From branch to branch a bird leaps
The beating of its wings strikes my heart

4.
Your share of the coming wave is its foam
There is someone who fills your heart with clouds

5.
The bee won't sit on my shoulder, although I heard it calling my name
Its idea of me is the same idea that will lead to its death: a break with the past

HASSOUNA MOSBAHI

Escape to Andalusia

TRANSLATED BY WILLIAM M. HUTCHINS

After the blue train had traversed rugged hills and mountains and cut through long tunnels, Andalusia's sun shone down brutally, and on both sides of the track spread groves of olive and orange trees, vineyards, and fields of sunflowers. Andalusian villages appeared, and their white stucco houses clustered together like huge eggs. Beautiful pots of flowers hung by their doors and windows as the blue train sped toward Córdoba: "far off and solitary."*

In my orange notebook I wrote: "I am escaping to Andalusia. I feel it is the only land that understands my sorrows and pains. No other land grasps the depth of my tragedies. Elsewhere tyrants scorch the earth and vegetation, stifle hymns of freedom, crucify lovers, and spread loathing and devastation. Only beloved Andalusia can shield me from their evil. Oh Andalusia! I enter by a different route – not that of the ancient Muslim conquerors, who arrived tired, exhausted, and weakened by wounds. I enter it wishing only to penetrate the depths of my soul and perhaps comprehend the devastating pain that has long tormented me, exactly as Ibn Khafaja al-Andalusi complained:

A man like me seeks another man
Who searches in himself for his self.
I want nothing, not memories, not homesick longing, not lamentations over ruins.
Oh, Andalusia, restore composure and tranquility to my troubled soul.

The train reached the station in Córdoba at 3 p.m. The heat had peaked and immediately reminded me of the heat in Kairouan at that time. American tourists with huge backpacks panted in the corridors and waiting room. I recalled Hemingway and his love for the impoverished Spain of his era, a Spain soaked in the blood of its sons during its civil war. I remembered his novel *For Whom the Bell Tolls*, which I read during a summer as fiery as this one, while I cursed an insignificant Arab author who had told me that Hemingway was a "superficial" writer.

I took a room in the first pension I found on leaving the station. A beautiful woman with wheaten complexion and intensely black hair opened the door for me. She reminded me of women from the old families of Kairouan. I washed and stretched out. In less than an hour,

---

* Federico García Lorca: "Song of the Horseman"

I rushed outside, eager to explore Córdoba. I had not gone far, though, before I felt the sun's arrows affecting my brain. So, I decided to return to the pension to wait for the evening. Then I would lose myself in Córdoba.

I quickly traversed the modern city, since nothing distinguishes it from other contemporary European cities. It has broad streets, grandiose banks, towering buildings, hamburger joints, and coffee shops that blare noisy, American music. Without my having to ask anyone, my steps led me to the Guadalquivir River, which suddenly glittered before me like a giant sword. In the distance, on the outskirts of the city, I saw windmills that the Arabs left behind them and that Don Quixote later thought were fierce knights challenging him to a duel. They were surrounded by the green plains of Córdoba.

I sat on a wooden bench beneath a tree that offered luxuriant shade and wrote in my little notebook: At times I feel that rivers recount history better than citadels, temples, pyramids, and museums, better than even the books of historians. With their ceaseless movement, rivers inspire in us the idea that they are the strongest link between past and present, that they carry in their waters secret emotions that bygone peoples and nations expressed in festivals and mourning rituals. This is true for the Nile, the Tigris, the Euphrates, the Volga, the Rhine, the Mississippi, and the Guadalquivir.

After a brief rest, I walked along the bank of the river till I reached the old city. The moment I entered, my spirit fluttered like an ecstatic bird. I was overwhelmed by the fragrances of the flowers, the beauty of the Andalusian women, and the ancient history I had longed for. I walked along tranquilly, pausing before honey-coloured doors and blue windows and balconies decorated with garlands of flowers.

On my right, a door suddenly opened, and a woman in her fifties looked out. She wore a summery, flower-print dress. I nodded to greet her, and she smiled. I used sign language to ask if I could see her house. Her smile broadened, and she showed me inside. The house resembled the traditional houses of Kairouan and Fez with its courtyard of rose-coloured marble and the four doors opening onto it. There was a fountain in the centre and a small orange tree. Every wall was covered with pots of flowers. A boy, who wore glasses and who was around ten, was leafing through a book filled with drawings. In one corner of the courtyard, a beautiful girl was weaving something. I felt I was in a little park filled with water, light, and shadows.

Hassouna Mosbahi

I remembered reading in a guidebook that the residents of Córdoba, in the middle of every spring, hold a festival they call "The Courtyards Festival," when rich and poor alike decorate their homes with flowers. At the end of the festival, an award is given to the person with the finest courtyard. It upset me to recall that residents of Kairouan and the Medina of Tunis neglect their ancient dwellings or sell them for absurdly low prices, because they "aren't contemporary enough," or so they think. Oh, how deformed and sick modern civilization is!

It isn't difficult to find the Great Mosque in Córdoba, since all the streets and alleys of the old city lead to it. I entered this mosque through the "Milk" Gate – Postigo de la Leche – and found myself in a vast courtyard filled with palm, cypress, and orange trees. From there I entered the sanctuary and began to roam among its gleaming columns and beneath its domes and arches. I was stunned by the splendour of the mihrab, which is decorated with mosaics, and the minbar, which is made of ivory and precious woods. My humble devotion was exalted then by the beauty greater than I had seen in any mosque before. As the German poet Rilke said: "Beauty is the beginning of terror we can barely endure." It occurred to me then that the heavy candles mentioned in old history books would have been burning and that three hundred servants would also have lit incense of ambergris and aloes wood and ignited the scented oil of thousands of lamps. Then I felt myself – body and spirit – dissolve into that magnificent spiritual atmosphere and sensed I was just a speck in that awe-inspiring space. When I left the mosque, I was tired, and my soul was exhausted. I plodded along as if I had just trekked a far distance over a rocky road.

I entered a small coffeehouse opposite one of the mosque's gates and rested my elbow on the arm of the chair. For a time, I remained downcast. Then I realized the young waiter was looking at me with interest. So I asked for a glass of water. After I ordered a second and a third, the young man asked me: "Where are you from?"

"Tunisia."

"From which city in Tunisia?"

"Kairouan."

"Oh, Kairouan . . . Fez . . . Córdoba."

At that moment, as if a ray of light had pierced my mind, I saw the long road that had started in Baghdad and Damascus and then passed through Kairouan, Fez, and Córdoba. It was a route that great adventurers, scholars, and people searching for the secret of existence had followed. It was Ibn Arabi's route and Ibn Khaldun's. It had been followed by Ibrahim al-Mawsili, and Abu al-Hasan Ali ibn Nafi' (who is known as Ziryab), as well as Lisan al-Din Ibn Khatib, who said:

I feared the heat a little, but refreshing breezes blew from the Guadalquivir as the streets and squares filled with great crowds.

Young women of Córdoba – as rowdy as fillies in springtime – emerged with their hair hanging down, and the air was scented by their perfumed brown bodies.

I sat in a small coffeehouse, swimming in a flood of light and love.

During this Cordovan evening, which caresses my body softly and calmly,

I offer you Cordovan flowers and the laughter of lovesick brown-skinned women.

I offer you these perfumed breezes and this gleaming Andalusian moon.

Then that Cordovan night grew larger and more extensive, and I lost myself in the type of beautiful ramble that captivates me in the cities with secrets and mysteries I love to discover. Now I imagined that all of Córdoba was dancing and singing. As flamenco music was audible everywhere, young men and women began to dance, stamping the ground with their feet. Sweet tunes resounded, and svelte bodies twirled and twirled and twirled, until I felt they were rising and revelling before evaporating into the vastness of space. From time to time, mournful songs were also heard, apparently recounting stories of love and longing in the red land of Andalusia.

In my orange notebook I wrote: I review in my imagination the great people of Córdoba: Abd al-Rahman al-Dakhil, the man who built its power and importance, Abu al-Hasan Ali ibn Nafi' who organized its life and dedicated its nights to music and singing, Ibn Zaydun who wandered in its gardens and meadows crazed by love, the passionate and rebellious princess Wilada bint al-Mustakfi, Ibn Hazm who taught its residents the language of passion and love, Musa ibn Maymun and Ibn Rushd who commented on Greek wisdom, and the poet Luis de Góngora, whom Velázquez painted with dramatic alternations of shade and light. On this splendid night, they rose from their graves. Now they were hugging each other in the streets and squares, listening with boundless happiness and bliss. Oh! When will camaraderie return to hearts in Arab lands, which have been depleted of love and peace.

At a certain moment I sensed that the night, like the sea when the tide is rising, was becoming rowdier and brisker. Warm waves dampened flaming bodies that had sung and danced till fatigue exhausted them and dancers collapsed at last on the shore of the dawn, which had begun to scale the horizons with its rose, violet, and gold.

* * *

I arrived in Seville one Sunday morning and found a room in a pension managed by a man in his thirties. The beauty of his bronze-complexioned wife so dazzled me that I tripped twice while climbing the spiral staircase.

The city was almost deserted. Coffeehouses, though, were teeming with American tourists, and I decided to avoid the city centre. I walked down empty streets in the brutal sunshine till I finally reached Seville's Fine Arts Museum. I passed about an hour there enjoying paintings by great Spanish artists of the Classical Period: Zurbaran, Murillo, El Greco, and Seville's renowned native son Velásquez.

I ate lunch in a local restaurant that specialized in preparing fish dishes in the Andalusian fashion. Near me sat two very annoying French tourists. The man had a large, bald head and a swollen chin. He chattered nonstop about trivial matters, eager to demonstrate his detailed knowledge of Andalusian history and its historic landmarks. When he noticed that I was reading the French newspaper *Le Monde*, he raised his voice and began to rehearse his knowledge as if lecturing a dim-witted student. His wife was thin and had a large nose, which resembled an overripe banana because of all the freckles on it. She wore a sun hat and from time to time asked her husband a pointless question to encourage him to continue jabbering.

So, I consumed the fish quickly and returned to my pension.

I slept soundly till five that afternoon when I ventured out into the city again. I took a seat in a small café shaded by trees to wait for night to fall. I wrote in my notebook: Seville is deserted this Sunday. I roamed through it in the blistering sunshine to experience what life is like here. Now I'm sitting in a small café waiting for nightfall.

At approximately six-thirty, evening breezes stirred to sweep away the day's silence and its lethargy. I walked toward the river and strolled in the Alcázar gardens. There I met a French philosophy student who carried in her bag the poems of Lorca and some novels by Gabriel García Márquez. She told me: "A year ago I decided to learn Spanish and now I speak it fluently. I love the language because of Lorca and Cervantes." The sun had seared her skin till it had turned the colour of fresh-baked bread. Her face was as small and round as a doll's face. She added: "I've been wandering around Spain for more than a month and have no desire to return to Paris before September. My boyfriend left me in Valencia and went back to Paris. He can't stand long trips. More than once he got fed up with the Spanish and called them cruel. I think he's stupid." We sat near a fountain, and she told me about her travels in Andalusia. "I spent a week with the Roma in Granada. They're good people. I danced with them. I slept in their houses that resemble caves. I love their sad songs that recount their sorrows and wanderings from country to country. A Romany boy fell in love with me, and I toured Alhambra and the Generalife gardens with him. I may go back there to see him before I return to Paris."

I found a seat in a café near the church and ordered a small carafe of sangria. A brown-skinned beggar girl who was around eight and had unkempt hair made the rounds with an outstretched hand, saying nothing. She ran her tongue over her lips, and it was clear that she had no idea what she was doing. From time to time she would pause and glance at a woman who leaned against the wall opposite her. When the sun began to set, a short elderly man stood in the square and began to play sad songs on a guitar.

I wrote in my orange notebook: I wander with the herd, penetrating deep into Andalusia. Now my soul strays in worlds I've never experienced before. I flee from hardhearted people, from the patronizing voice, from the "heroic" leader, from professional poets, from the pimps of corrupt regimes, from phony critics, from "objective" researchers, from journalists who suffer from verbal diarrhoea, from authors of romance novels, from croaking litterateurs, from academics with bellies bloated with bilious eloquence, from men with bushy beards who promise paradise, from creators of empty slogans, from those who undermine revolutions, from those who pretend to weep for "Lost Andalusia", from criminals who affect weird styles of dress and appearance . . . I flee from all of them. I escape like a bird fleeing from a metal cage, a poet from the tyranny of a dictatorial ruler, or a pupil from a tedious lesson. I feel that I am seeking the light and ridding myself from the burdens of the past and from a worm-eaten cultural heritage covered with spider webs and that in Andalusia I am born again: as clean and pure as water gushing from a spring.

As night began to spread its flower-scented, star-studded curtain over the city, I was overwhelmed by a desire to sing and dance in the streets while embracing love-sick maidens. I wandered through the ancient district of Santa Cruz, where the streets and squares were full of people. When flamenco music resounded, two girls of about thirteen started to dance. They kept on twirling and twirling until they collapsed in a pool of sweat. I didn't return to the pension until three in the morning.

* * *

I left for Granada one cloudy, overcast day in a train packed full of American tourists, most of whom were in their twenties. They talked all the time in loud voices, wearing earbuds for a Walkman while holding a bottle of Coca-Cola. I had to change trains in Bobadilla, where I encountered an old woman I had seen at the station in Seville. She was shouting and chattering as her saliva spattered the air. She seemed intent on guiding travellers, but they didn't understand anything she said. She wore a dirty grey blouse with blue trousers that were torn at the knees. Her face was furrowed with wrinkles, but her eyes were as cold and glassy as a plastic doll's.

After the Bobadilla station, there were fewer groves of olive trees, and on both sides of the tracks stretched barren, chalky plains punctuated with eroded hills. Cattle were thinner, and houses looked desolate, as if they had been abandoned long ago. The train passed dismal villages devoid of flowers and joy. Then the earth gradually grew green again, and groves of olive and orange trees and fields of wheat and sunflowers were more frequent. The morning's thick cloud cover cleared, and the train entered Granada station toward noon.

The colour of a ripening pomegranate, Granada rests in a hollow surrounded by the lofty Sierra Nevada Mountains, the mountains of the moon. Something about this setting may remind a visitor of Marrakech, because even when you swelter in the fiery August sunshine you can see snow on the distant peaks. Since I was keen to learn about the city's kings of the Nasrid (or Ahmar) Dynasty, I left the room in my pension after only about half an hour.

I set out on the Gran Via de Colón, which cuts through the modern city. It was almost deserted. Shaded by trees, old people and African migrants were selling parasols and trinkets. Some of them had grown sluggish from the heat and boredom. I made my way to the historic Carrera del Darro, which was also deserted. I found silent, narrow alleyways and houses decorated with flowers as in Córdoba and in the Santa Cruz district in Seville. The only sound was my footsteps on the stone of the pavement. I saw an intoxicated old man leaning against a wall in a corner. He grasped a wine bottle that was half empty. Spittle dripped over his bushy, dirty beard. His eyes were red and swollen, like pieces of rotting liver. When he noticed me he muttered something, and I approached him. Then his tongue moved, but he didn't say anything. I handed him a coin and left him. Gradually, beautiful, luxurious houses gave way to low-standing houses devoid of beauty or flowers. They were inhabited by the poor and by Romany people. Suddenly some brown-skinned children appeared and trailed after me inquisitively. When I started to photograph them, they fled. A beautiful woman there was hanging up laundry on a roof. She smiled down on me, and I smiled back. After I walked past her, three adolescent girls wearing summery dresses appeared from a doorway and began to laugh softly and coquettishly. They started to approach me, but a voice shouted at them from somewhere, and they ran away, chirping like happy birds.

Along an alley I discovered a coffeehouse so small it could accommodate only ten patrons. The manager was a woman with large hips, gold teeth, and a broad, brown face heavily coated with makeup. She wore a black, loose-fitting dress, and her eyes were wide and sensuous. She was smoking avidly. A man, in his fifties, wearing a white shirt with blue trousers, sat in a corner. His grey hair was carefully coifed. He was drinking and smoking silently. I ordered a beer, which the woman placed before me. Then she walked a few metres away. After she had studied my face for a long time, she said something I didn't understand, and I gestured to her that I didn't know Spanish. She laughed and said something to the man. He didn't reply, not even a word. Then I remembered a woman called Zuhra in Kairouan. She was a sexy dame who inflamed the hearts of young men who arrived from the countryside hungry for sex. I thought this woman in this impoverished neighbourhood might be Romany. In any case, she certainly knew the secrets of both the old and the young here. When she noticed that I was gazing at her tall body, she laughed naughtily and winked her right eye. Once more she addressed some remark to the man in the corner, but he remained silent, focused on his glass and his cigarette, which was smoldering. When I left that Romany coffeehouse, the Sierra Nevada mountains were drenched with the red of sunset.

I spent my first night in Granada in the Albaicín district. *Oh, Albaicín!*

On a white marble plaque was inscribed, in blue letters: "Here was the Arab Quarter of Albaicín." That alone sufficed to remind me of everything that had happened there in the distant past. Equally evocative were the twisting and intersecting alleys fragrant with jasmine and rose blossoms, the trellises for grape vines on the white walls, the sedate old women sitting at their doorsteps, the loving expressions of brown-skinned maidens, my desire to kiss the mole on the cheek of the waitress in the Plaza de Fátima, the young men and women dancing to Flamenco music, the sighs of lovers down a deserted alleyway, the plump man who was ecstatic when he learned I was a "Moor" (in other words an Arab), and the full moon, which looked like a giant jasmine flower. *Oh, Albaicín!*

the Albaicín, photo by Samuel Shimon

Before I went to bed, I wrote a friend: "For the first time, my friend, I can announce that I am one of the happy Arabs. Yes, among the residents of Albaicín, with people who don't speak Arabic, I have sensed that their spirits, dreams, laughter, eyes, houses, songs, and dances are Arab. I do not feel at all like a foreigner among them. I even think I would like to live the rest of my life among them. Oh! How exquisite a night is in Albaicín, my friend. People dance, sing, and make merry in the plazas and on the streets without fear of censorship or of the police – unlike in our Arab cities. They own their space, my dear, and enjoy it, whereas we are denied our spaces, because the ruler has swallowed everything, leaving us not even a small space to exercise our freedom. We bridle our desires and our dreams. Thus our beautiful plazas have become depressing squares. Albaicín, my friend, seemed larger and more spacious that our entire Arab world, which extends from the Gulf to the Atlantic Ocean. In all our countries we have lost the taste for happiness, joy, and freedom. I wonder whether the last Arabs are the residents of Albaicín in Granada?

One scorching morning I walked to Alhambra Palace, because I didn't want to take the bus. I ambled slowly through the ancient markets and beautiful gardens, where there was plenty of shade thanks to the clustering and concentration of trees. As I walked along, I revelled in the songs of the birds and the purling of the streams flowing toward the Adra or Darro rivers. When I arrived, I found myself in a long queue of people waiting to buy an admission ticket. The tourists there were of many ages and nationalities, except for Arabs. I began my tour in the maze of Alhambra Palace: the courtyard with the large orange-coloured dome. I toured the Hall of the Ambassadors, where emirs sat to settle disputes between people, beneath the huge hand carved into the boulder and raised skyward as a symbol of justice ruling the physical world and the hereafter; the Court of the Myrtles, the marble pool, the men's diwan, the flowers painted in the queen's boudoir overlooking the gardens, the baths of the princes and princesses, the Court of the Lions, the Hall of the Abencerrages, and the Generalife gardens: water, light, roses. A young French girl told her mother: "*Maman, il paraît que les Arabes avaient du goût.*" ("Mummy, the Arabs seem to have had good taste.")

At the end of my tour, I collapsed on a chair, and my head spun. As my feet burned, my soul plunged into valleys of despair. A desire to weep overwhelmed me. Hot tears soon rolled down, for I felt a bitter isolation, an extraordinary sense of being orphaned, of being a solitary orphan who had lost everything and who had betrayed the beauty he had created, the beauty of his soul that had once yearned for love, light, and enjoyment, for which he had substituted instead: hideous ugliness, hatred, and a culture of death.

Late that evening I set out again for Albaicín to bury my sorrows there.

Four days later I left Granada beneath the blistering August sun, and headed for the sea.

ABDELKADER BENALI

To Tangier with Emmanuel

**A SHORT STORY TRANSLATED BY
SUZANNE HEUKENSFELDT JANSEN**

Photo by Abdelkader Benali

I had removed myself from the party hubbub to catch my breath. As an uninvited guest one should not stand out too much. I saw myself as a 'one': thinking about myself as an 'I' made me feel vulnerable.

Disappearing every now and then was the cork on which this risky enterprise floated. It was an enjoyable wedding, by the way: fun guests, a superb buffet and a genuine cocktail bar. I was thoroughly enjoying myself on this sultry June evening.

No one would notice an extra guest if you behaved yourself – I eased my conscience by viewing my risky operation as a form of anthropological fieldwork. When would someone with my background ever be at a Dutch wedding? Never. I learnt a lot: I saw how people dressed, what the etiquette was and how the different sexes related to each other. I heard their language and languages, their non-verbality. It was surprising. I enjoyed the beauty I saw, the feeling of an evening out at the opera.

I began to understand the expression 'one wedding begets another'. Nonchalantly clutching my glass of Prosecco, I watched which way the beatific cat would jump. Dispensing the odd nod, not flirting too conspicuously with this or that lady, putting off wicked things for as long as possible, suppressing the thoughts about it, suiting the action to the word is something I could do at the close of the market and so on . . . Then they would be for the taking, the ogling women with a weakness for brown eyes. Flirting fine; going along with it less so. I had real trouble keeping up my lies in the face of a beautiful, excited angel. Those who bare all must dare to bare all: lies will no longer suffice. In order to avoid the awkwardness of it all I usually proceeded home alone. In very rare cases I gave in and afterwards regretted it deeply. After exchanging body parts I felt burdened with an enormous sense of guilt. The reek of fraud enveloped me. The game knew its limits.

I had attended many a wedding in this way and nothing had ever happened to me. I had behaved myself impeccably: a true gentlemen, almost to a fault. A quick glance at my watch told me we were approaching midnight. The happy bridal couple would soon retreat. I ordered a beer at the long hotel bar. Two empty stools along, a man roughly my age was drinking whisky. Whisky gave me a headache; whisky has to be consumed in the right doses, which is what my aversion must also have been to do with. I did not have the patience for it; one day in another life. I had noticed this striking young man before. He danced. Flirted incessantly with the women – grabbed the odd one by her waist, pirouetted and romped on merrily. I guessed him to be a little older than me. In between dancing he slapped wedding guests on the shoulder and threw them a laugh. Why he did this was not immediately apparent to me. It seemed as if he found it important to be seen by everyone. I attributed his shamelessness to drink.

I downed my beer in one swig and ordered another. The speed with which I glugged it gave me a feeling of triumph. As if that nonchalant gesture showed that I understood the art of glorious living. I was in control of the drink, was enjoying it, I had earned it. It made me strong. The excitement made me especially thirsty. The adrenaline pumped through my body; there was nothing for it but to drown the stress in drink.

"Hey you, you there!" the whisky drinker called out to me. I opened my eyes. The barman topped up his Glenfiddich. 'Mr. Glenfiddich' I dubbed him: giving someone a nickname was an instant means of staying in charge. It gave me the feeling that I was in control of him. In between my secret and his curiosity lay Glenfiddich.

His call had an undertone of aggression. Interrogator, snooper, sceptic. He kept inspecting me, waiting for a response. I raised my glass and made a toasting gesture. I did not fancy fielding awkward questions from a young man who was the worse for wear. The second beer went down pretty swiftly, too. What was to stop me from actually getting completely plastered?

"Family of the bride?" he continued, in a quiet tone this time. Clutching his glass, he shifted one stool towards me, and dropped onto it. Straightened his back.

"A friend," I said: "I'm a friend who's delighted that his friend has finally found happiness. One of those nights that the world is good, almost perfect. And you? Do you call yourself a friend?" By asking a bold counter-question I kept him even more at bay. Pulling the initiative towards you, letting the other person hold forth, feigning in-

Abdelkader Benali

terest, a great deal of nodding, of raising the glass, clinking, drinking and carrying on as if it were the most natural business in the world. Feigning casualness was everything.

"I'm also a friend," he said. "From college. Mark's a diamond." So they knew each other well.

"Mark's incredible," I said. He threw me a penetrating stare as if I had made an unhealthy remark.

"How come I've never seen you before?"

"I live in Australia these days."

"What's your name?"

"Carlos."

"Oh, it's you," he said. I drank my last sip of beer. Put it down and go.

"Yes, that's me," I replied.

"He talked about Carlos."

"That must've been me."

"Carlos was ill. Did not have long to live. Terminal."

"I survived," I said. "I'm alive. It was a miracle." Nothing for it but to dive into the lie at full depth then.

His bow tie hung untidily around his neck, his brown hair was wet and sticky from dancing, you could easily spot the curvature of his muscular shoulders through his dinner jacket, the result of many push-ups. A distinct presence, in everything my counterpart. He slid towards me, glass in hand. "Okay, brother, *finita la commedia*. Carlos is dead. So either you are his reincarnation, or you sauntered in hoping for a night of carefree boozing. Either way, you've got guts." I folded my hands on top of each other, very piously, as if the wrongdoing he had attributed to me applied to someone else. "I saw you standing there, ogling the women," he went on. "You sneaked in."

Breathe deeply. That thirst again. That fear.

"I slipped in because I love this – gate-crashing someone else's

Photo by Abdelkader Benali

party. Is that a crime? As far as I know I'm not harming anyone. If you don't approve, I can reassure you: I'll be gone in two minutes." There was only silence from his end, and he wasn't drinking any more. "Brother, you and I, we're doomed. But where I become glum, you make something out of it. Can I get you a drink?"

What started with a glass and a few civilities ended with us still talking to each other at the close of the night. We left the premises arm in arm, pleasantly intoxicated. Shaking him off was going to be difficult. He did not stop talking. About his exes – there were many; about his financial successes – he had had quite a few; about his travels – he had travelled so much. The fact that he secretly admired what I had done must have had something to do with it. Sneaking in like that, hanging out as the smooth operator. Having guts was held in high regard by him, shamelessness even more. There was more that bound us. We showed off our knowledge of literature. We went from Heinrich Heine to Graham Greene to Kafka to Isaac Babel to Montale to Céline to Saba to Borges. To him, literature was a villa you could raid; he shared his profits with the pathos of a burglar who has netted his haul.

"You and I," he called, "we're going to do projects. Set up an orphanage in Malawi. Build a hotel in Andalusia." But first a taxi had to be found to get us home, which was no easy feat as all the taxis had been booked. So we walked many kilometres, singing soldiers' songs from the British colonial army to ourselves until we reached the busy main road. "Drop him off first," he said to the taxi driver, "and I will pay for the rest of the trip." When we said goodbye we agreed to see each other the following day in the city.

The first time I invited him to my student flat, he pounced on my books. At that time I did not know anything about his work as a copywriter for an advertising agency in Amsterdam, which was busy creating a name for itself with slogans for full-fat milk, AIDS prevention and the Dutch national football team. "The most important part is transforming the product into a mystical entity. An icon that wants to be kissed. That gets them moving. That gets them kissing."

He told me this later. Seeing the books made his eyes glint in an almost maniacal way. Like a child in a sweetshop. "Why didn't you tell me?" he cried. "This is what binds us. Literature with a capital

'L'." He snatched a poetry volume by the Russian poet Joseph Brodsky from the table, dropped onto my worn leather sofa and began to quote in an exaggerated tone, increasingly loudly, with heavy emphasis.

I opened a bottle of wine. We drank, we read out to each other and at the end of the evening, or at the beginning of the night, I confessed to him I was working on a novel. "With a cover and page numbers and real chapters?" he said.

"Stop it." I said.

"Have you got something? Show me." His look could switch. I reached behind me with my hand to where, on a shelf, I had the first thirty typed-up pages of my novel. What had got into me? Was I going to show this guy, whom I had barely known a few months, the document I was working on in the utmost secrecy? I saw myself pushing the bundle of papers forward with a lot more bravado than I thought I had in me.

"Son of illiterate parents and then this," he said. He struck the paper with his hand. If he wanted to draw attention to something, if he found something staggeringly amazing, he swung out with his hand. And when he got bored, he also swung his hand. The world was not safe from his hand.

"What's it about?" he asked.

"It's about a girl," I said.

"Love?"

"In places," I said.

"So she really existed?"

"I want to write literature."

"Jesus, you're such an elitist prick. Such airs. Just say what you have to say, man!" Should I have noticed that he could not stand me being busy taking my ambition seriously? Yet what he pierced was my attitude, not my dream. Even after having withstood his hail of sarcasm, I continued to believe in what I did. Believed in it more than I ever had.

"I'm also writing a novel," he said.

"Sir is writing a novel," I said.

"The few people who've read it are impressed."

"Family? Friends?"

"Devotees," he said.

"I also want to read it," I said, "I'm a devotee. A devotee of everything that's good."

He began to laugh at me. Took another sip. "If it's good, I wouldn't be shouting it from the rooftops, would I? The reader must think it's good. I only write. Fuck it, everything."

"Would you like someone to read it?"

He screwed up his eyes in a scowling way. "Suddenly getting all polite to seduce me into letting you have a glimpse of my work? Patience, *mon ami*. Patience."

We had to get to Tangier. His obsession, not mine. For me Tangier was a geographic location, not a literary one. He talked, I listened. He, Don Quixote, looking for literary redemption; me, Sancho Panza, whom he could fool into believing anything. Kerouac. Paul Bowles. William Burroughs. New names to me around whom hung an aroma of borderlessness, cultural confusion and drugs. American outsiders, self-declared loners, who had found in Tangier a second, third, fourth or spiritual home.

With the knowledge I have now, writing from this cramped prison cell in Malaga, he must have found me naïve: naïve like Sancho Panza, but without his guile.

He liked the fact that I presented myself as a *tabula rasa*: it gave him the opportunity to dump on me all the knowledge and literature he had acquired about this city of white cubes. Talking involved drinking, because talking made him thirsty. I joined him in this – seeing someone drink makes you drink. I wondered how we would come by our alcoholic refreshments in the Muslim country that is Morocco. "Tangier is a port. A port without cafés and rough dives is like a courtesan without lovers. Come on, drink up!" He found it tremendously suspect when I did not drink with him: abstinence for whatever reason was a form of betrayal to the Cause.

"Those American buccaneers went to Tangier to smoke hash. To do some serious drinking. To go after the boys and girls."

"Doesn't sound very edifying."

With his hand he lashed out at my face, as if he was about to give it a terrible smack of malice and loathing. It happened so quickly that I had no time to duck away.

"I'll explain one last time, Calimero! Deliverance is found in disorder. The intellectual mind stands in its own way. It needs to be put off its stroke in order to get moving. They descended on Tangier to throw overboard the orderly side of themselves."

"Travel that far for a joint?" He saw that I had not learnt my lesson yet. It was time to take a beer from the chiller cabinet; the colder the drink, the more slowly he would drink it. Each sip a *bitter*.

"The best hash in the world is sold in Tangier. The hash farmers take it to the city in person. They're not stingy. Hash is common food. It's difficult for an artist to remain himself. The role society forces him to play destroys him. It's better to write than to die. Job done." His face contorted, as though someone had sprinkled lemon juice in his eyes.

"Isn't Tangier a bit too rough for us?" I pointed with my bottle of beer at his polo shirt, the cashmere scarf draped around his neck, and the brogues. "We'll be out of place. And that feeling paralyses me. Maybe the Tangier you're talking about exists only in your head. And that's where it should stay. A story that can never be fully written out as it doesn't have a clear beginning or end."

"Villain!" he shouted: "You're a coward! If we want to change the world, we have to force ourselves to be someone in that world."

The cheapest ticket we could find took us to Casablanca. To prepare, we had watched the film *Casablanca* with Humphrey Bogart. That meant we could give the city a miss without a sense of guilt. On the plane, Emmanuel filled me in on the colonial city that was built on top of ancient Anfa. At some point I stopped listening; many tales would follow.

From the airport we took a taxi to Casa Voyageurs and from there the first train to Tangier. It was a train that, judging by the Dutch and French information signs, had done duty in Belgium. The last section took us past the Atlantic coast. Emmanuel slept. I looked outside and drifted off into my reveries. In the river delta that ended up in the sea, where the water became brackish, cows were standing motionless. The animals seemed to be ablaze in the intense late-afternoon light, as if they had eaten fire. The ocean disappeared behind the hills to appear a few kilometres further along in the shape of the Mediterranean. The train crawled towards its terminus.

The wide beaches were dirty; two dogs lay sleeping under a torn and broken parasol; the few Western seaside visitors whom I detected lingering among the locals dragged their fat stomachs like a status symbol. The pinched swimming briefs and big Ray-Ban sunglasses turned them into caricatures of a Westerner. Some of the men were surrounded by street urchins. They stood frozen like statues and looked down on the hustle and bustle around them.

Emmanuel shone with excitement; the mix of the Mediterranean sun and manifest despair made him shimmer.

"What a dismal place," I said.

"Sir's not wasting any time spouting his opinion. What did you think, that you were going to Venice where everything is scrubbed and polished three times a day? Our continent has been hijacked by cleaners. Euphemistically, these cleaners are called managers. But I know better. Behold true existence here. No fuss and frills; culture is nature here."

"Tourism is ultimately luxuriating yourself in the misery of others. And feeling that things are pretty good at home. Tourism is the only thing that can save us from self-hatred." I said.

"You should write that down and publish it," he said. "And ask money for it. Get out of my eyes." He fully opened the half-open window so that he could hang out of it with his round head. "It's thirty degrees in the shade. I'm seeing camels. I'm seeing palm trees," he shouted into the carriage. "And you call this a dismal place? And you want to write? Loser."

"I'm not going to lie down on that beach. Have a look at what's prancing around on it."

He opened his rucksack, pulled out the bottle of Johnny Walker Black Label he had bought in the Duty Free shop at Schiphol, raised it to his lips and immediately passed it on to me. "*L'chaïm*, as the Jews say: to life."

The train had come to a halt again, its wheels groaning and screeching. If the building we saw on the horizon was the station, we did not have very far to go. The train doors had been opened. We could get off with our backpacks and find our way to the guesthouse. Emmanuel stayed put. He seemed to be waiting for something.

I stopped after one sip. He raised the bottle once more to his lips. And again. People filed past, they jumped out of the carriage and carried on their way. He smiled at three Moroccan students who edged past in order to get off the train.

"*Bonjour, bonjour, Mesdemoiselles, vous-êtes tangéroises?*" The smile of

Photo by Abdelkader Benali

his brazen approach had immediate effect.

"*On est de Casablanca.*"

"*Vous passez des vacances à Tanger?*" They smiled at each other as if he was irrelevant. "*Nous, on vient de Hollande, de Rotterdam.*" He pointed to himself. "*Moi, je m'appelle Garcia.*" He pointed at me: "*C'est tête de couchon est Carlos.*"

Once the train had stopped at the port of Tangier's tiny station, he flung his head out of the window and called after them: "*Bonne chance!*"

"Why did you compare me to a pig?" I accused him. "In Islam a pig is an unclean animal."

"But you *are* an unclean animal."

We fended off the calls from the taxi drivers who wanted to take us to our guesthouse. Emmanuel did not have a good word to say about them. Judging them on their appearance, he relegated them to swindlers: "They think we're suckers – stupid Americans who, because of their fear of the unfamiliar, are an easy target for the shiny wide boys."

The guesthouse was at the end of the steeply ascending street. We collapsed onto the worn-out mattresses. "Keep your clothes on in bed," said Emmanuel, "otherwise you'll get crabs. I don't think we'll get much sleep anyway. This city is for nighthawks."

In the morning we walked the entire upper city, through the ghetto's twisting alleyways to the boulevard where we looked for a spot between the seaside visitors. He gave Moroccan dirhams to the beggars who approached him. They placed their hands on their hearts and let us go.

"Why do that, all this generosity?" I asked.

"Pure tactics. I've given them money, made them happy. The misery of their existence has been bought off. If I'd walked straight past them, I would've been given the evil eye. And we wouldn't want that, would we?"

"I didn't know you were superstitious."

"I'm not. But they are, and that's what counts. What's more, they won't ever bother me again. Everywhere south of Granada, once it's been given, it's given."

We spread our towels on the beach.

He applied suntan lotion to his pale skin. He kept his sunglasses on. He had no intention of going swimming. He studied the beach, whistling through his teeth.

"Samuel Beckett once walked on this beach, did you know that?"

"But there's nothing doing here," I said, "what did Beckett see in this city, or Bowles?"

"They didn't see anything in it. Maybe you're seeing too much."

A few hundred metres along stood a few dromedaries, their owners nowhere to be seen. Much closer by were beachgoers who darted in and out of the water, as if it housed a water monster that snapped at their legs.

"Look who's sitting there," said Emmanuel, pointing into the distance. At a respectable distance from the camels sat the three girls we had met on the train.

"Tricky, tricky, tricky," said Emmanuel.

"What's tricky?"

"The fact that there are three. You can't break through that. It would've been much easier with four, they would split up and no one would feel lonely. But whichever two may like the look of us, they'll never abandon the third. Girls' *omertà*."

Emmanuel began to wave.

"What are you doing? They can't see us anyway."

"They can see everything, they know we're sitting here." One of the girls – in my eyes the most beautiful – waved back. Emmanuel dropped his hand. "Pfff, it's so hot." He jumped to his feet and ran towards the mounting waves.

In a few days' time, our visit would be over. We were beginning to run out of money. Emmanuel had borrowed some from me; in the upper city cafés he also paid the drinks for the intoxicated men he got talking to.

Towards the morning, Emmanuel staggered back to our room. He reeked of tobacco, hash and alcohol. A few hours later he rose briskly, roaring with energy. It was our last day, time to leave. "Let's hit the town, let's go to the hotel where the girls are staying. If they know that we're leaving tonight it'll increase our chances of a quick fling."

We had to check out. If we paid fifty dirhams extra we could leave our rucksacks in our room. Emmanuel asked me if he could borrow some more money. That evening we were going to take a ferry across the strait, a journey that would last less than an hour. In Tarifa, we would take the bus to Malaga, from where we would continue by train. I had to lend him all his travel costs. We walked through the city, aimlessly it seemed to me, but it did not make the city any less interesting. We climbed steep streets to discover new neighbourhoods on the other side of the hill. He stopped in front of an apartment building. "This is where it is."

"What?"

"Paul Bowles's apartment. This is where he lives. Come on, let's go and say hello. Aspiring writers who know his work inside out."

"Not me, I don't."

He slapped me on the shoulders. "Your readiness to take your place in life is everything, my friend."

We rang the bell at the door with the nameplate 'P. Bowles'. A middle-aged man answered the door. He had to disappoint us, Mr. Bowles was too ill to receive people. Outside, we were scrutinised by the local boys. Emmanuel smiled at them. One boy asked where we came from. "The Netherlands." The boy asked if we wanted to buy hash. Emmanuel brushed them off.

We continued on our way to the hotel where the girls were staying. The receptionist had to disappoint us, they were out. "*Dommage,* what a shame!" Emmanuel exclaimed. We entered a bar. Emmanuel ordered a beer, I stuck to Fanta. He ordered another beer, knocked it back and grabbed my knee. He mumbled something and got up. "Time to go."

At the guesthouse, our backpacks were waiting for us at reception. The receptionist was not there; a young boy had taken his place. He did not look at me. Emmanuel gave him a fifty-dirham tip. We picked up our backpacks. "Careful," said Emmanuel.

After a few hundred metres we sat down at a small restaurant. Emmanuel looked at my backpack, at me, and at the people passing by. The boy he had given a tip passed our table. "There he is again," I said.

"Our guardian angel," said Emmanuel. We ate our last meal on Moroccan soil. In that restaurant I decided I did not want to stay in touch with Emmanuel. Distance did not have to stand in the way of our friendship. But I did not want to see him anymore. I asked if he could watch our backpacks and went into the bazaar to buy souvenirs for the girlfriend I was going to have.

En route to the port I was following him. The boy from reception had popped up again and led the way, guiding us into the port and telling us which queue to join. Emmanuel was sweating in the heat; I was sighing under the weight of the backpack. The crossing was wonderful. I thought I spotted dolphins. The air was fresh, Tangier disappeared behind us, the Spanish coast approached rapidly. In that small stretch I felt life could go in any direction – any direction would be good and positive. Emmanuel had become seasick; he spent the entire hour hidden in the toilets. The ferry docked in Tarifa, the doors opened. Emmanuel was standing first in line, his face blank, empty, helpless. I called out his name, but he did not turn around. The crowd began to move and poured around the officers of the Guarda Civil who were standing ready with their dogs to intercept drug smugglers. On our side the light seemed brighter, almost blinding. The dogs made a beeline for me, trapped me in my movement, snapped at my backpack. The officer stopped me brusquely. I said I was with Emmanuel. They asked me for my papers. When I began to think more clearly again, I realized I had lost everything. I never saw Emmanuel after that.

MONIR ALMAJID

A Syrian Japanophile

TRANSLATED BY SAMIRA KAWAR

The serenity of Matsuyama, which has a population of barely half a million, and my residence in its suburb of Toon-City, have turned me from a mere visitor into a "Japanophile" over the past few years. It's as simple as that.

MONIR ALMAJID

On board a small Nippon Airways (ANA) aircraft at Matsuyama Airport in Japan, the only thing I could hear is a few passengers whispering. The calm was dubious and ritualistic. The air stewardesses, looking like wood pigeons in their grey and pink costumes, moved around helping to put hand luggage in the designated places, bowing and kneeling when talking to any of the passengers. Suddenly they disappeared.

A few minutes after take-off, they reappeared, having changed into different clothes – dresses, aprons and thin scarves – and tied back their hair back into small buns. The reason for doing all that was to offer some refreshments, which took fifteen minutes. They came back to collect the plastic glasses, which took another fifteen minutes. Five minutes later, they had changed back into their uniforms, as the captain was announcing preparations for landing.

The serenity of Matsuyama, which has a population of barely half a million, and my residence in its suburb of Toon-City, have turned me from a mere visitor into a "Japanophile" over the past few years. It's as simple as that.

Metropolitan Tokyo captivated me for a no more than a few days: its beautiful buildings; its wonderful landmarks; its famous Shibuya Crossing, which attracts hundreds of thousands of tourists, and the imperial palace, like a castle, surrounded by walls and moats. Even the very large Ginza neighbourhood only attracted me for a few days, just because as a visitor, I was and will always be unable to fathom this city and interact with it. It is so huge, that even those who live in it only know very small parts of it. That is why I am so fond of Matsuyama. It is small, but it has all the hallmarks of the big cities, albeit on a smaller scale.

Toon-City is situated on the main road that links Matsuyama to the eastern part of Shikoku island, and further afield to cities like Kobe, Osaka and Kyoto. It is 18 kilometres from the centre of the city. It has noticeably expanded over the last decade, particularly the area between where I live – where my veranda overlooks Toon High School and from where I can clearly hear the students clamouring during practice in the sports hall and the sound of the ball as it bounces, or very out of tune music by some student practising the piano – and Ehime University Hospital. Four years ago, the area was mostly taken up by green fields, but it has turned into a neighbourhood of modern, western-style villas. Its trees and flowers are still young.

As is usual when new neighbourhoods are built, it has attracted a hairdresser, a dentist, a pharmacy, and of course a convenience store. And I mustn't forget to mention three public gardens, each the size of a large apartment.

The River Shigenobu flows to the east. The strength of its flow depends on the rainfall over the many surrounding mountains. As it flows down through Matsuyama, it merges with the River Ishite – and as is the case with all the world's rivers, which end up flowing into oceans, seas and lakes – the merged rivers flow into the calm waters of the Seto Sea, which fully resembles the Japanese: calm, but you never know what is hidden in its depths.

Sakura cherry trees have been planted on both of the river's banks. They usually bloom in the last week of March for no longer than ten days. I have become attached to the Sakura season, and it has become a link between me and Japan and its people.

The flower is the country's emblem, and it appears in its feminine pink wherever you may look: in restaurant dishes and sweets; in the colours of clothes, films and magazines, young girls' smiles and pupils' bags, hundreds of thousands of books, television programmes

Matsuyama, photo by Monir Almajid

Autumn by Shigenobu, photo by Monir Almajid

and traditional Kabuki theatres.

Historically, people became enamoured with plum (ume) blossoms during the Nara period (710–794 CE). Just like cherry trees, plum trees bloom at the end of March for three to four weeks, and the flowers have an attractive burgundy colour. But the love affair with plum blossom did not last long because in the Heian period (794–1185 CE) cherry blossom attracted more attention, probably because of the story surrounding their short life span. The imperial court and bourgeoisie began to celebrate the flowers with what became known as the Hanami festival or cherry blossom festival, and were quickly followed by the Samurai warrior class.

However, the love of cherry blossom did not spread to the common people until the Edo era, when Buddhism spread, and spiritual and ritualistic dimensions were incorporated into the Hanami tradition. People planted cherry trees everywhere – along river banks, on mountains (where families would visit them during the day and lovers at night during the flowering season, and the local authorities would work to build cafés, lavatories and flood lights) and in the yards of homes, companies and schools.

During the many wars that the country fought, the sakura, or cherry blossom, was used as a nationalist and propaganda symbol to stiffen the resolve of fighters, because it symbolised the "Japanese spirit" and "warriors at the ready, like the abundant cherry blossom ready for dispersal". Even Kamikaze pilots drew the sakura symbol on their aircraft before devastating the US navy at Pearl Harbour.

Once peace was restored, and the people of East Asia were released from their hell and men tended towards a rejection of war, the sakura became the flower of flowers, a religion and a passion. One cannot understand that passion unless one is there to see, feel, hear and smell the phenomenon.

Hanami is a tradition that has been imbued with sanctity, but also with uninhibitedness. People go out in a sakura mood, with their barbeque equipment and lots of beer, choose a tree to sit beneath and take snapshots before alcohol takes control of their minds. It is then that the Japanese get over their reserve and inhibitions. After a bottle of beer and a few shots of *saké*, their voices rise a little. Nevertheless, they never forget to clean up the place afterwards. Cleanliness is a chronic obsession.

On several occasions when I was roaming around and photographing the beauties of nature, I was invited to have a drink with them, and they would say "*Campai*". Invariably, they would express curiosity at my presence and where I had come from, all in the broken English they had learned as students.

The main street of Matsuyama is about a kilometre away from my flat. It is packed with cars, as well as restaurants on both sides. Two of those restaurants are Udon and Soba, and there is a branch of the cheap Joyful chain, where I have eaten several times. The coloured menu shows the number of calories in every meal. When I order a beer (282 calories), the waitress very politely asks if I am driving, because if I am, she will refuse to serve it to me. You must have a zero percentage of alcohol in your blood if you are driving.

Fuji Grand Mall is four kilometres away, and houses shops, fast food restaurants and cafés that attract young people, the grilled meat Yakiniku restaurant, and even an Indian restaurant from which the scent of curry and infernal pepper waft.

As you approach the city centre, you catch sight of Matsuyama Castle, which crouches like a mythical eagle on a hill that is as large as a mountain. It was built by Kato Yoshiaki in 1603, and is one of the country's most famous castles. Around two kilometres to the right of the castle is another famous landmark: the Dogo Onsen hot springs bathhouse, a traditional building with its steel-like compact structure. It is more than a thousand years old, and is considered one of the oldest and most famous bathhouses in Japan.

I have always been bothered by the overhead electricity wires. They are not haphazard, as they are in Middle Eastern cities, but they nevertheless detract a great deal from the enjoyment of viewing the city, particularly since they hinder my passion for taking photographs.

At the entrance to the Okaido covered shopping arcade, you come across the luxury Mitsukoshi department store to the right, with its back walls overlooking the back streets. The Okaido arcade meanders slightly, connecting to another shopping arcade, known as Gintengai, and then leading to the other department store, Takashimaya.

I usually wander around those two department stores to while away the time before having dinner at one of the many restaurants situated along the side streets. That is when I indulge in the particularly pleasurable pursuit of observing people. Many of the passersby are residents of the city, and most of them are teenagers. The girls are bow-legged, hovering around in groups. Some look like porcelain dolls, have pencil-thin figures, ivory-coloured complexions with faint traces of veins visible, and black flowing hair. But once

NEXT ISSUE

A CHAPTER FROM

THE MIRTH OF THE GODS: 40 DAYS IN INDIA

BY MAHDI MUBARAK

WINNER OF THE IBN BATTUTA AWARD FOR TRAVEL LITERATURE

TRANSLATED BY
SUNEELA MUBAYI

they open their mouths, they reveal teeth that are lined up in a way that does not fit their beautiful appearances. I have always been surprised by the low number of people in this country who wear braces as teenagers to correct the alignment of their teeth. Other girls have roly-poly bodies that are full of McDonald's fast foods, which are spreading like a cancer throughout the country. It is a culinary tragedy for a people whose bodies have been historically distinguished by their leanness. Although the clothes they wear follow Tokyo's crazy trends and the *Kawaii* (cute) culture that is being marketed these days, they are modest, unlike those worn by western girls who distract men's concentration by generously displaying their bosoms.

The young men also move in groups, their brows covered by long thick hair. Mostly out of conceit, they avoid exchanging glances with the girls.

When I hang around there, or when I ride a train jam-packed with students holding their mobile phones as though they were lifejackets, or with employees in black suits with black briefcases under their arms looking exhausted and overcome by tiredness, I also provoke other people's curiosity. That is almost certainly because of the dearth of foreigners and tourists in the city. Even panting dogs walking alongside their owners stop to look at me.

Following the principle of "Eat local wherever you are", I try as much as possible to visit Japanese restaurants, or those that offer *Washoku* (literally, Japanese food), which is the name most in use for all Japanese food, whereas western food is known as *Yoshoku*. The former is internationally known as healthy cuisine, UNESCO considers it part of human heritage, and it is both simple and complex. Its method of preparation, which is permeated by sensitive traditions, taste, and charming presentation, is simple. But its many ingredients render it complex. One of its most distinctive features is the *Umami* taste (which combines sweet, bitter, salty and sour tastes to give you the fifth taste). The Japanese have been familiar with it for hundreds of years, but the rest of the world have only got to know it in the last thirty years.

The first part of the word *Washoku*, "*wa*", signifies one of Japan's many names. It also has another meaning that can be summed up as "harmony". The second part of the word, "*shoku*", means "food". Moreover, based on Chinese Kanji characters, the word also means "ingredients by combining all the senses". More important than such difficult terms is the fact that the Japanese kitchen is seasonal. It utilises the ingredients available in each season to create an appropriate meal, and then they must be served in a very elegant manner in the appropriate ceramic dishes. As for the service, that is a Japanese trademark.

Western food invaded the country during the Meji era (1868–1912) when western traditions began to influence the nation. Restaurants began to serve meals that included strange elements, such as butter, ketchup and Worcester sauce, and this also helped to make way for Asian cuisines (Chinese and Indian in particular).

At luxury *Washoku* restaurants, you don't sit around a table with other customers. You get your very own spacious "apartment", with its own bathroom, and with a window overlooking a garden where there are small waterfalls. Here you are exposed to rituals similar to those of secret societies. Here is an example that in general fits most restaurants:

I arrive at the allotted time of my reservation, and the waitress, wearing a kimono, leads me with short, sprightly, dainty steps to my "apartment". She kneels before me to inform me of the evening's events, then gives me a piece of paper that details the number and types of dishes that I will be served, and the kinds of *saké* that will accompany each one. Then she withdraws, shutting the door behind her, leaving me to take in the surroundings. Moments later, there is a knock at the door, and she asks permission to enter. She comes over and kneels once more to serve me *saké* and some small spicy starters. Then she leaves, bowing as she does so.

On one such visit, as soon as I finished drinking the imperial drink (served in a cup), I heard her requesting permission to enter, and to my great surprise she entered carrying a small jug of *saké*. How did she know I had consumed the first one, rather quickly perhaps? The entire evening unfolded in that way, not only with regard to the *saké*, but also with the various dishes. As soon as I finished one, the next one would arrive. What strange timing was that? How could she know that I had finished one dish so she could bring in the next? I had to find out the secret. At ordinary restaurants, the waiter watches you from a distance, then comes and serves you. But in that restaurant, the doors were closed and no one could watch you. At the end of the evening, I asked: "How do you know that I have finished a cup of *saké* or a dish, so you can bring the next one?"

"The sound," she answered cryptically and mysteriously. Then she explained: "The sound an empty cup makes when you put it down on the table is different to the one a full cup or a half-full cup makes. The same applies to putting chopsticks down on an empty plate."

You will get even more of this kind of treatment at the three Michelin Star Hyotei restaurant in Kyoto. The restaurant is more than four hundred and fifty years old, and dates back to the fifteenth generation of the Yoshihiro Takahashi. Three waitresses served me at that restaurant, and were waiting outside to welcome me when I arrived in a taxi.

History is an absolute must in the country of the sun. Since its establishment, the restaurant serves its famous *Tamago* (egg) dish, which used to be considered a rare delicacy at the time. The secret recipe of *Dashi* stock, which they mix in with the eggs, cannot be duplicated. *Dashi* is the DNA of the Japanese kitchen, in exactly the same way as Kyoto is at the heart of the imperial cities.

Because I have mentioned Kyoto, I must refer to another example of maintaining tradition and the revival of the Japanese spirit: When Kyoto was the imperial capital, providing it with fresh fish was a big problem, because it was around seventy kilometres away from the coast at its nearest point, and transporting fish there took a long time. In order to keep it from spoiling, particularly on hot summer days, they used to preserve it in salt. Now, in keeping with tradition, they salt and pickle it for a short time to get that special taste, even though the fish is very fresh since modern transport allows speedy delivery. A mackerel dish known as *Bo-sushi* is prepared in this way. A self-respecting chef will avoid using thin plastic strips to separate the fillets of fish, resorting instead to aspidistra leaves that are cut into different shapes and forms that conjure up images of Hans Christian Andersen's paper cuttings. Aspidistra belongs to the same plant family as asparagus, and the leaf resembles the blade of a machete. The rice used in this recipe must always be of the Japonica type, which is a short, round grain, and provides a cohesive consistency as though the grains have been formed of some secret kind of glue.

My repeated trips to Matsuyama have begun to yield exciting discoveries, including new restaurants, some replacing ones that have gone bankrupt. The competition is unbelievable, and prices are a third lower than in Tokyo. I have absolutely no reservations about eating anywhere, even at modest-looking restaurants that have small entrances covered by two pieces of cloth. I have become adept at recognising ingredients without remembering their names, but every time I go, I am prepared to experience new flavours.

The city's restaurants are like a mini United Nations. In addition to the very popular Italian restaurants, you come across Chinese, French, Spanish, Vietnamese and Korean. There is also one owned by a young Armenian man from Turkey who has still not managed to present Turkish cuisine well, probably because it's difficult for him to find a specialised chef. So he sometimes turns his restaurant into a night club. At other times, he brings in a Japanese dancer who learned to belly dance in Cairo. The point I am trying to make is that the owners of most non-Japanese restaurants that are managed by Japanese people have cleverly succeeded in adding some twists to their menus so that they appeal to Japanese tastes, but they have not forfeited the main character of the dishes. For example, my Danish Friend Thorbjorn Andersen, who runs a Danish restaurant outside the city of Kochi, offers very low-fat traditional dishes, although fat content is one of the distinctive features of north European cuisine.

However, chef Hiro Aoe, who hails from Osaka, is an exception to that, and I consider him to be a "food activist". He offers solely a genuine Tuscan menu at his restaurant, and insists that the local soil is very conducive to growing Tuscan vegetables, and so collaborates with local farmers.

If you want to avoid formal restaurant protocols, you can choose something completely the opposite. My favourite such place is Izakaya, because of its simple, genial, slightly noisy atmosphere. Izakaya can be compared to a Spanish Tapas bar, or to a Greek, Turkish or Syrian restaurant. It serves a collection of small dishes that are not necessarily exclusively Japanese, and the main focus is alcohol, particularly *saké*.

Or, take Italian restaurants, for example. The number of restaurants that call themselves Italian equals, or even exceeds, the number of Japanese restaurants. You can order pizza and spaghetti with a Japanese flavour. This might sound like an insult to the Italians, but just ask anyone who has tried them. Here in Japan, they seem actually more appetising and better tasting.

Then you have rice and curry. Although this is an originally Indian dish, the Japanese have turned it into the favourite at restaurants for families, and for children in particular. They have reduced the amount of spices, particularly the very hot ones. If you wanted to support the erroneous impression that reduces Japanese cuisine to just sushi, you would have to find a sushi restaurant– and they are actually few in number.

When I dine with my friends, I say "*Itadakimasu*". I practise this habit, which is a necessary one if you visit the country and eat with its people. The word is pronounced without the "u", and it has several meanings. Because I like simplicity, I will just mention one such meaning: "Bon Appetit". But it also conveys a wider sense of thanks to the farmer, the fishmonger, the butcher, the truck driver, the shop attendant, the purchaser and the chef. A Japanese person may learn the word "*itadakimasu*" before learning the words "Mama" or "Papa", and it is a very necessary word. If you pronounce it well, you will please your Japanese friends. Why not, since it signifies such nobleness?

I could, in fact, continue writing about Matsuyama, which, when I travel there, feels like going home. That is what it has become to me. But I will end by saying a few words about Toichi Takahashi, who is a master *saké* maker, and represents the Japanese spirit of dedication, hard work and attention to the minutest detail.

Takahashi hails from the Akita prefecture, and is seventy-four years old. He says: "If you want to understand how *saké* is made, start with a rice field." He has discovered that it is important to use the least amount of fertiliser possible in the soil in which the rice is grown, as that increases the proportion of protein in the rice, changing its consistency, and giving it a cloudy appearance. He is never hesitant to share the experience he has gained over the past half a century, and he has become the undisputed *saké* guru. His main motto, which he himself explains, is "Don't manufacture, raise".

When I go to the Izakaya, I look for Saiya Takahashi *saké*, which is the brand that has won the highest number of medals in competitions, and it sets me on fire like a cigarette.

Talking of cigarettes, it is strangely the only place where I can tolerate the smell of cigarettes, and float like everyone else, in their smoke.

Photo by Nouri al-Jarrah

SAID KHATIBI

Sarajevo

I walk behind my shadow...
and repeat a children's song

TRANSLATED BY PAUL STARKEY

SAID KHATIBI

The road from Zagreb to Sarajevo is a little over four hundred kilometres. I studied the road map in the morning and reckoned that the journey would take about five hours, taking account of the time spent stopped at the Bosnian border guard post. I took a quick glance at my things and threw them on the back seat of the car, leaving the hotel owner counting banknotes without paying attention to anything going on around him, not even my heavy steps along the corridor linking the reception to the exit. I started the engine and headed south, towards another life, another horizon, a mixture of cultures and ethnicities that did not belong to the clumsy Union on which the marks of premature ageing had already begun to appear.

Sarajevo tickles the memory like a distant floating song, constantly appearing and disappearing. It is a face divided into two halves: a Muslim east and a Christian west – a natural artistic canvas, spattered with the blackness of the years of the two World Wars and then of the Civil War, the most prominent and repeated headline to dominate the news broadcasts in the mid-nineties.

In the spring of 2012, I remember that I had been extremely keen to see the film *Djeca/Children of Sarajevo* during the Cannes Film Festival contests. Later, though, it seemed to me extremely superficial and I could see in it nothing but an imaginary, truncated Sarajevo. This made me change my mind at the time: I did not attend the press conference that followed the film screening and I abandoned the idea of interviewing the film's director herself. However, I retained the wish to visit the city itself one day to see its quarters and buildings at first hand. Now I was heading for the Bosnian capital with just snatched scenes from old TV footage and photo albums in my mind. I was thinking of the faces of people who looked just like me. They were like something from the Algerian world I had come from.

I don't know how my attachment to Sarajevo started, before I had visited it or even thought of visiting it. It was just there in my imagination. I seemed to know it and its people. Perhaps it was because of the wound that was still apparent on its face; the tragedy of the war that had given it a dress that was not its own. During my years of childhood in Algeria, at the age of ten, we would be at school and in the scout troop, and we would sing for the children of Sarajevo. Like them, we lived to the rhythm of death and blood and im-

Said Khatibi

ages of daily murder. This made it a natural thing and us developing an affinity became a historical necessity. Of all the Balkan cities, Sarajevo seemed to me like a piece of the heart. No journey in the region would be complete without it.

I left Zagreb in the morning as I had arrived, in the morning under a nonstop drizzle of rain. I followed the city signs and directions carefully, so as not to lose my way to my destination, Bosnia. I passed through the towns of Kutina and Novska. Along the sides of the road stretched large fields, hemmed in by high mountains. We could only see a few people there, for machines had provided the human hand with some relief. Before reaching and crossing the border between the two countries we had to pass through a region called Slavonski Brod, which contained the nearest crossing point open to travellers. As I got nearer, although the map showed that I was no more than about 50 kilometres from Bosnia, it was noticeable that the Croatian authorities hadn't bothered to put up any sign with the name 'Bosnia' on it. Everything gave the impression that the road simply led from Croatia to Croatia rather than another independent state. Relying simply on the map I had with me, I reached the Croatian crossing point and took no more than five minutes to pass through it before entering the territory of Bosnia and Herzegovina.

The Bosnian border guard took my passport and turned it over this way and that. He tried to read what was written in French and Arabic then asked me: "alžirski?" [Algerian?]. Yes, I replied, without actually speaking. He looked at the number plate of the Slovenian vehicle then called a colleague: "Look, look! He's an Algerian!" "He's a Muslim. Look at his name!" his colleague replied. I didn't interrupt their conversation. I simply continued to look at them and at the people crossing the border on foot or motorcycles, on their way to Croatia to shop and buy essentials from the stores, then go back to their villages to re-sell them. They were crossing to the EU before returning to their homes, which were a long way from the politics of Brussels. The same officer looked again at the number plate while I stared at him the whole time, saying nothing. I remember that someone in Slovenia had warned me against going to Bosnia in a vehicle with a Croatian or Serbian number plate, while it was also necessary to avoid being in Croatia in a vehicle with a Serbian or Bosnian number plate as the three neighbouring countries had not yet patched up their differences.

Finally, he gave me back the passport without a stamp. I said nothing to him, for I was eager to see a country that had nested deep in my heart. Just a few metres past the crossing point, the scenes I had left on the other side began to change rapidly. The roads were potholed and ancient, in urgent need of repair. They were full of bumps and hollows in all the wrong places, reminding me of the state of the roads in Algeria. In Algeria, we can find a bump on a highway or two bumps one after the other on a small side road, and if we ask why we will hear the typical answer: "God knows!" On either side of the road, I could see villages scattered here and there, usually containing houses and other buildings that looked as if they were owned by people of good social standing. People in the northern region of Bosnia in the 1990s knew how to make the area inaccessible and protect it from armed conflict, and the area knew comparative stability by comparison with the towns of the centre and south of the country, as well as the areas bordering the Republika Srpska.

The first station we passed on the way to Sarajevo was the small town of Doboj, which is the most important railway junction in the country. This good fortune allowed it to become the headquarters of the national company for rail transport. Historically, it was the stronghold of what became known as the Yugoslav Partisans, founded by Marshal Tito to confront Italian Fascism and German Nazism. The same army subsequently assumed a different role, namely the formation of military units to combat the plan for Croatian secession. Doboj belongs geographically to what is called the Republika Srpska of Bosnia, which together with the Federation of Bosnia and Herzegovina forms the State of Bosnia and Herzegovina.

It was midday when I reached the middle of Doboj. I thought of grabbing a coffee and sandwich and resting for a bit. I parked the car near a restaurant and café, went in and asked the waiter: "Do you take euros?" "No," he replied. So what to do? He suggested that I change some currency. Where? There were no exchange offices in the vicinity. He pointed me to a petrol station near a small hotel. He told me there was a young man there who changed euros into Bosnian marks. I headed over and asked for him but didn't find him. He was travelling on the other side of the river, in Croatia. I couldn't eat a sandwich or drink a coffee as they refused to take my euros, so I was forced to return to the car disappointed. I was now just hoping to eat and drink as soon as I arrived in Sarajevo, having obviously first found an exchange office.

Entering the capital of Bosnia and Herzegovina was like entering a city that was both subversive and unique. Everything in it aroused inside me a yearning for previous places I had known and lived in. The first place I had to ask for was Baščaršija, the noisy centre of the city, where I had reserved a room in a small hotel. I passed through some side roads and a passerby advised me to follow the course of the river Miljacka, which divides the city east to west into two halves. It is both the hydrological identity of Sarajevo and its historical calling card, for on its banks the well-known events of the summer of 1914 took place, involving the assassination of the Archduke Franz Ferdinand, heir presumptive to the Austrian throne, and his wife, the Duchess of Hohenberg. This was the immediate cause of the outbreak of World War One. The operation was carried out by a Bosnian youth, Gavrilo Princip, who was only twenty years old at the time and a member of a nationalist organisation called Young Bosnia.

History muttered on the riverbank as I crossed over, watching the

Sarajevo, photo by Nouri al-Jarrah

signals and looking for someone who would give me directions to where I wanted to go. After a few minutes among a gentle crowd, I found myself in the Baščaršija quarter. I was entering it from Baščaršija Square, or Pigeon Square as some people call it, as the pigeons flock there every day to pick up scraps while tourists take photos. Then I walked up towards a hill opposite, looking for a small hotel. I had forgotten to draw a map of how to get there, as I usually do with places I am visiting for the first time. "Don't look at maps too much in Bosnia: ask people if you want to go somewhere in particular!" my Slovenian friend had told me. I stopped in front of a hotel on the road, went in and asked a slightly plump girl with bright red hair, who spoke fluent English, for a hotel called Talal. She looked me up and down and then said she'd never heard of it before, though the hotel, after I had reached it by asking some passersby, was no more than 300 metres from her own hotel. Perhaps she didn't respond because she didn't want to be of service to a rival or was jealous of losing a customer to a small hotel that could hardly be seen. When I went into my room in the Talal hotel, there was nothing to suggest that we were in a three-star hotel: a small bed, ordinary cheap furniture, and a large window overlooking a narrow residential street. No other services were on offer apart from breakfast, which was basically coffee with milk, a glass of juice and two boiled eggs. I wasn't that bothered, for I'd chosen the hotel to match my budget for the trip and I needed to be as economical as possible to complete the journey.

I put my things on the bed and went down to the reception area to ask the young, slim receptionist for the nearest exchange office. Before she could reply, I also asked her whether I should pay for the room now or at the end of my stay. She told me I should pay later and without giving any further details told me that the exchange offices were in Baščaršija, and that was that! So I had to look and ask again. It wasn't too difficult. The city centre knew how to welcome foreign tourists and there were exchange booths on every corner. The local currency was losing value against the currency of neighbouring Croatia and I could live well for three days on a hundred euros, which would pay for food, drink and accommodation,

In Baščaršija I smelled the smells of the Algiers kasbah. The history of both areas went back to the Ottoman period and both were built on a hill, which in the first case adjoined a river and in the second the sea. Baščaršija means Trade Street in Turkish and it has remained to this day a street crammed full of shops, restaurants and cafés: the focal point of a city that stays awake night and day and almost never sleeps. The credit for building the city and for its fame belongs to Husrev-bey (1480–1541), who ruled for a full seventeen years during the reign of Suleiman the Magnificent – the latter of whom had an enormous influence, both internally and on Europe. Husrev-bey built a great mosque bearing his name, which is considered one of the most beautiful mosques in Sarajevo and the whole of the Balkans, and which together with his tomb enjoys visits from pilgrims and tourists, Muslim and non-Muslim alike.

I changed some euros and headed for the first restaurant I could find. I sat down and without thinking ordered *ćevapčići*, a famous local dish prepared with meat in a traditional way and usually wrapped in a local bread, accompanied by spices and small pieces of onions and sometimes by cheese. *Ćevapčići* is almost a daily fast-food dish in Bosnia, the equivalent of *karantika* in Algeria or *lablabi* in Tunisia – a popular snack and the signature dish of the Balkan kitchen in general. Some historical sources say that the same dish first appeared during the period of Ottoman rule and was subsequently developed by the Serbs, then settled on the tables of the inhabitants of Sarajevo, before later being taken, thanks to migration, to Western Europe, where it became especially common in the restaurants of Germany and Austria. There is nothing better than a Turkish coffee after eating, to recover one's breath and provide relief from a journey of about five hours. To sit on a restaurant pavement, to eat, drink, watch the passersby and listen to words and voices in a foreign language puts the visitor at the heart of the action, helping him prepare to enter the fray and pass through the gateway to all that is obscure and marvellous in the city.

As I got up and paid the bill, the city was adorning itself for me as tiredness flowed through my body. I decided to take a short walk in no particular direction, wherever my feet took me. I went into areas with stone pavements and felt the walls of buildings that bore the aroma of history. I smelled their ancient odours and conjured up something of an imperfect memory of the quarters of Constantine and Annaba, as well as my own small city in the south. In Sarajevo distances disappear and the details of life come together and disperse again. Life there, despite the uncertainty that goes with it, makes those who live there feel self-confident and proud of the past. Life does not appear as raw as it does in Zagreb, or as predatory as in Paris, but rather humble and honest in its love and hatreds (if any), pliant in its continuity and concerned for its sons rather than itself. Sarajevo lives on the memory of the names of those who have passed through it, on the chronology of human folly that it has lived through and still lives until today. It is the comma separating amazement from confusion.

The following morning, I left the hotel around eight o'clock, eager to have a walk around the city. Rain had washed the face of Sarajevo during the night and reminded her that autumn was approaching. The first image that confronted me in front of the Talal hotel, behind a small, crumbling wall, was a row of about ten graves lined up one after the other. Muslim graves with white headstones, bearing the name of the Almighty in green. Graves and the smell of death in the middle of a residential area, in front of a hotel which announced itself as a tourist hotel. But the surprise would gradually disappear when we subsequently realised that graves and mass burials were an established part of the general appearance of the city, a landmark that could not be detached from its other landmarks. In the capital of Bosnia and Herzegovina, life and death are neighbours, arguing and making up at every moment. Death embraces life while people continue their daily lives, without bothering or at least without mourning or renewing their sorrows. In a public garden in front of the Bosna Bank International building on Marshal Tito Street (or Marshal Tita in Bosnian), near the Iranian Cultural Centre, is a graveyard containing the bodies of adults as well as hundreds of child victims, their names written on a collection of slabs to perpetuate their memory. Not far away is the mosque of Ali Pasha, at the entrance to which we were met by an area of martyrs' graves. "Most of them fell during the siege of Sarajevo", I was told by Rajab, a waiter in a popular café.

The siege of Sarajevo is still considered the longest and harshest military siege in modern human history. It lasted about four years without any break (from 4 April 1992 to 29 February 1996), for after the declaration of independence from Yugoslavia, the city found itself at the mercy of Serbian troops. According to some official estimates, the number of victims of the siege exceeded ten thousand, in a period when Sarajevo was daily exposed to hundreds of missiles, which targeted government institutions and other civilian buildings and resulted in the destruction of almost all the city's vital sectors. I was young then and it wasn't enough to sing for Sarajevo and the children of Sarajevo. We would go around the shops, asking people for contributions to send to human caravans, which were supposed to be directed to the children of the besieged city. We showed solidarity with a world far from us, while we lived in a situation that was no better than theirs: murder, killings, terror, and daily intimidation in an Algeria that was living in the shadow of an unprecedented futility. "People were burying their dead in the nearest place possible. They didn't dare move further away for fear of the enemy bullets," Rajab added. The victims' remains stayed where they were and were not moved elsewhere after the war. So in the space of four years Sarajevo became a mass graveyard open to the world, and remains like that until today. Despite the blackness of the image in its symbolism, the visitor does not feel the sort of terror that runs through the body when visiting other graveyards. The gravestones were spread out in rows that were repeated so often in a single area that it seemed quite normal. The bustle of daily life and the solitude of the dead came together, side by side.

At one evening gathering, at around eight o'clock, an enormous screen was erected in front of a café in the middle of town opposite a mass graveyard to watch a historic World Cup game, which brought Bosnia and Slovakia together in the course of the 2014 World Cup heats. A quarter of an hour before the start of the game, the general atmosphere was marked by a state of joy mingled with some hysteria. The dividing line between the graveyard and the pre-match celebrations was no more than ten metres. In the ninety minutes of the life of the match, the scene turned into a massive arena of nationalist songs and emotions. When the match ended in a Bosnian victory, taking it nearer to qualification for the Brazil Mondial, the dead nearby almost awoke from their sleep to share their joy with the living, in a scene even more hysterical than that experienced by Algeria when it qualified in Omdurman in 2009. Young girls and old women came out and everyone joined in singing and dancing in the street until morning. The presence of a lot of women attracted my attention. It seemed to me that they had become more interested in football than their counterparts in the Arab states, for example. But Nur, a Bosnian woman in her mid-thirties, laughed at this idea, adding: "They don't understand much about football. They usually come to try to catch a man, taking advantage of the enthusiastic and celebratory atmosphere." I couldn't make out whether she was speaking seriously or sarcastically. The important thing was that every woman who was there would have a share of the happiness: be that a man or a dance or a feeling of pride at seeing the country moving closer towards the greatest world sporting event for the first time in its history. Several times I tried to look deep into the eyes of the girls of Sarajevo and to grasp their trains of thought. They were beautiful, usually with milk-white skin, but they didn't look happy. The general situation didn't encourage the good life. On the basis of widely circulated statistics, the youth unemployment rate was more than 60 percent. And studying did not necessarily guarantee success, since both international and local official institutions refused to recognise the qualifications awarded by some universities and private institutions scattered throughout the city. To emigrate to a Western European country was a common dream, said Salim, a Palestinian in his fifties who had been working for more than ten years for the Kuwaiti Relief Institute in Sarajevo. "Where have the millions gone that were sent from Arab countries to rebuild Bosnia?" I asked Salim. "Where did the long kilometres go that a group of my colleagues covered in the quest to help the children of Bosnia during their elementary school years?" I asked myself. "It's true that millions were sent, but the purpose was usually to build mosques rather than spend it on development projects," he replied. Muslims building shrines and minarets, Christians responding by building all the churches they could, and Saddam in Iraq growing more entrenched year by year. Between the mosque of Gazi Husrev-bey and the Cathedral of the Sacred Heart there is a gap of a few metres, no more. And near them is the Museum of the Bosnian Jews, a small museum with specialised holdings of ancient manuscripts and illustrations detailing the chronology of the Jewish presence in the region. Three heavenly religions coming together under the sky of a single city in apparent peace and inner convulsions. In the street, in the residential areas and on the main thoroughfares, ethnic differences are hardly apparent. The hijab is not common among women and the provocative display of Christian symbols is not widespread. The biggest shared feature that brings together young and old, men and women, are the signs of the last war, which are difficult to hide from view. The city is haunted by the enormity of its recent past and sleeps and wakes to the hideous nightmares of the nineties, cleansing itself of fear by prayer in the mosques which surprise us in practically every quarter. On a visit at the time of the noon prayer to the Emperor's Mosque, dedicated to Sultan Mehmed Fatih, we confronted the deep roots of history. The mosque was built at the time of Isa Bey in the middle of the fifteenth century CE, only to be destroyed by fire and rebuilt in 1766. The mosque is composed of a single rectangular prayer hall, a dome and a minaret, which was destroyed during the war in 1992 and rebuilt in 2000. As is the case in Zagreb, prayer brings together men and women, the women praying at the rear without any curtain or barrier to separate them. Everyone enters through a single door and uses a common shelf for their shoes in a state of creative organisation with no room for ambiguity or lack of respect. The state of tolerance and solidarity engendered by the war years has acquired deep roots in present Bosnian society. Everyone has lived a common drama and everyone understands well the pain and suffering of the other. This is something that has strengthened and continues to strengthen social cohesion between the Muslims of the single country.

Beyond the walls of the city centre, the signs of the other face of Sarajevo begin. A simple, poor, difficult life, relying on just a little food to continue its existence. Behind the stylish tourist façade of

Sarajevo, photo by Nouri al-Jarrah

the centre, the margins are plunged in deep, vital contradictions. The average individual's income is no more than 300 euros. Opportunities to work and think of carving out a stable, independent life for the young are ambitions hard to come by and there are no possibilities for change. This Sarajevo hides its shame at its poverty in a glossy touristy image, which captivates visitors who come from a distance and those who don't know much about it.

In the shadows, disordered quarters and unpaved roads spread out, eyes looking for a better tomorrow that has been a long time coming. A young man dreams of a foreign bride who may give him an opportunity to emigrate and resolve his legal status far away from his quarter and his extended family – in Switzerland, France, Britain, America or somewhere else. Women sit and look out for the return of past lovers, cousins who had emigrated once but may perhaps come back to look for a second, 'legitimate' wife. An unsettled life ruled by possibilities rather than certainties, dominated by expectations and the futility of hope, in which the lowest social classes become even poorer while those with connections and interests continue to gain the greatest advantages. A desperate situation not much different from the Arab situation, for Bosnia, which is geographically European, often seems like an Arab fragment, with its chaos and the haziness of its ambitions. It fights the blackness of its situation with dreams, summoning disjointed fragments of a very distant past, of a time when it was considered the hidden paradise of the Ottomans, a tolerant and transparent homeland for Jews fleeing from Spain. It tends its current frustration by cultivating wishes and praying hard for the end of the period of austerity and the return of the liberating prophet who will shake from her the dust of injustice and insecurity, freeing her of the inferiority complex and split personality that have kept her awake for a long time. For she still lives with an internal rupture: Bosnia and Herzegovina as we know her is divided into three different regional entities: the Federation of Bosnia and Herzegovina, with its capital, Sarajevo; the Republika Srpska, with its capital at Banja Luka; and finally, the Brčko District. Divisions which did not satisfy the Muslims of the country (the Bosniaks – the majority), but which emerged from the Dayton accords (1995) in order to end the ethnic war in the country. The Muslims regarded them as unfair because they divided the country almost equally with a second party numerically smaller than they are.

Today I feel that I left a part of my heart in Sarajevo. I found in it something I have not found in other cities: tranquillity and a desire for deep reflection. A city which resembles me as I resemble it, to a point almost of identity: lazy like me, elegant, poor and proud of itself. Its districts, women and cafés have strong smells, which still tickle my nose, for Sarajevo flirts with the visitor from the moment of the first encounter, leaning toward him and drawing him as close as possible to herself so he may stay and never leave her. And if he leaves, he will leave with the intention of returning. Every story merges with every other in her daily life. The Balkans can only preserve their long history and stubborn present with a city that smiles like Sarajevo.

A chapter from *Jana'in al-Sharq al-Multahiba – Rihla ila Bilad al-Saqaliba* (The Inflamed Gardens of the East – A Journey in the land of the Slavs). Winner of the Ibn Battuta Award for Travel Literature 2015

Celebrating Kafa al-Zou'bi

In this feature, the reader will discover an exceptional novelist from Jordan, Kafa Al-Zou'bi, whom Banipal is proud to celebrate and introduce through three distinct texts. In a literary essay, Kafa Al-Zou'bi tells us about becoming an author, about the books and authors who have had an influential impact on her life and works. Then there's a chapter from her latest novel *Shams Baidha' Baridah* (Cold White Sun), followed by an excellent review of it by the author and fellow Jordanian, Fadia Faqir, who read it in the original Arabic.

Kafa Al-Zou'bi was born in 1965 in Ar-Ramth, Jordan, where she finished high school in 1984. That same year she travelled to Moscow to study the language before moving to live in Saint Petersburg (then called Leningrad) in 1987 and study for a BA in Civil Engineering at Saint Petersburg University. In 2006 she returned to Jordan. She is the author of five novels. Her third, entitled *Laila, the Snow and Ludmilla* (2007), dealt with the collapse of the Soviet Union and questions of Arab and Russian identity, and was published in Russian in Moscow in 2010. Her fourth novel, *Go Back Home, Khalil* (2009), written in Russian, has been published only in Russian. *Cold White Sun* is her fifth novel, and was shortlisted for the 2019 International Prize for Arabic Fiction.

Literary Influences

KAFA AL-ZOU'BI

The Bag of Wheat

My father never asked me the question that fathers often ask their sons and daughters: "What are you going to be when you grow up?" My mother didn't ask me this question either. I was the youngest of seven, with five older sisters and a brother. We lived in the town of Ramtha in northern Jordan, where we shared a two-room, stone and mud-brick house with our mother and father, neither of whom had learned to read or write, and who just barely scraped by. As was common practice in Arab societies, the people in our town never congratulated a family that had a new baby girl. Instead they consoled them with the words, "Everything God gives is good"!

Neither of my parents asked me or any of my sisters about our futures. The only decent future that a girl in our town could realistically hope for was to find a husband to provide for her. Consequently, my parents offered up fervent, humble prayers for the most one could possibly dream of – that the husbands would be well-off, kind and compassionate.

My two oldest sisters deviated neither from the town's established customs nor from my parents' dreams. Both of them dropped out of school to marry as soon as acceptable suitors came knocking at our door. But the other four of us, in our first act of rebellion, made up our minds to finish our education.

I think of human life as a dialectical text in which the individual produces and composes his or her reality, after which this reality reproduces and recomposes the individual so that together, they alternate the roles of composer and composed. Human beings produce intellectual, political, social and economic systems, then their lives remain bound within the context of these very systems. In our Arab world, these systems hem people in, restricting the range and development of their mental vision, and binding them with chains of illusion and fear. They form a text in which the Arab individual is doomed to incompleteness, whether in relation to God, who has predetermined their fate, or in relation to a tribal society now transmuted into a political and economic entity which, despite its civilized, urbane exterior, has yet to relinquish its tribal, patriarchal, male-dominated concepts and ways of thinking.

This dialectical equation in which objective reality and the individual recreate each other is a universal human phenomenon. It is also impacted by each individual's psychological makeup, instincts, will to survive, class struggles, and existential and philosophical questions. However, the Arab experience is uniquely marked by its ties to religion, its historical-cultural heritage, and to colonialism. Given this fact, the Arab woman lives within the subtext of her incompleteness as a female. This subtext is her prison-within-a-prison: her own narrow cell within the slightly more spacious prison of her society.

How are we to rise up against these two predetermined texts when – in keeping with the roles defined for us within them – we are expected to embody both the broader text that shackles society, and the narrower subtext that shackles the woman? In the context of our financially constrained family, we four sisters may not have asked ourselves this question in any explicit way. Even so, we did find an answer to it, not by clashing directly with our surroundings but, rather, by acquiring the tools that would enable us to enter the fray. And the tools were academic achievement and scholarships. This was our first step toward recovering a sense of identity in a situation where we were looked upon as deficient simply for reasons of gender.

When first the oldest, and then the youngest of our foursome won scholarships to attend college, books started making their way into our house. These books were like guests from a realm far removed from the world of the village, its scorching heat, and its soporific

Emily Brontë

Victor Hugo

noon hours dominated by the drone of flies that served as still another manifestation of boredom and stagnation. It was a realm alien to people who praised God morning and evening for every tragedy that afflicted them, and who constantly asked forgiveness for sins they were helpless to stop committing. Books of literature, poetry and philosophical inquiry, they were guests from a world where words were laden with meanings we had never encountered before, a world of words that brought cherished hopes of justice, equality, and change for the better.

When the number of books in those two mud-brick rooms reached a critical mass, one of my sisters used some of her scholarship money to buy some cheap metal bookshelves, and we went to work covering them with wood-patterned adhesive paper. There were creases in the corners, crooked lines, and gaps we had to patch here and there. But once we had arranged the books on those shelves, they were a library built from the finest mahogany as far as we were concerned, just the way, once we had attached our dreams to our day-to-day reality, that reality had seemed not only less forlorn and harsh, but downright presentable.

I began immersing myself for hours a day in the novels of Emily and Charlotte Bronte and in Victor Hugo's *Les Miserables*. I would wander about, lost with Dickens' waifs in dark, filthy alleyways . . . in distant worlds where I found that other people were persecuted and tormented like us, only in different ways. At that stage, of course, I wasn't ready for *One Hundred Years of Solitude* by Márquez or *The Brothers Karamazov* by Dostoyevsky, those two magnificent novels that I would end up reading time and time again with ever-renewed enjoyment and wonder. When, at around fifteen, I decided

LITERARY INFLUENCES

One Hundred Years of Solitude by Gabriel García Márquez

to read them for the first time, I was challenged beyond my ken and bored out of my mind. But I kept up the effort out of pride, counting the pages I had left, until at last I slammed the first book shut, followed by the second. (To hell with that! I decided.)

Not long afterwards, I picked up a pamphlet on Marxist philosophy – dialectical materialism and historical materialism. My sister the university student laughed at me. She told me it would be over my head. Maybe it was her mockery that made me all the more determined to read the book, although it was a challenge I don't know if I was up to. In any case, little by little, as I reread one paragraph after another, I began to grasp the logic behind Marx's explanation of Nature, History, and the laws that govern their conflicts and their dialectical evolution. The word "dialectical" sounded strange to my Arab ears, and it took a lot of practice before I could pronounce it, still less understand what it meant.

My initial understanding of that booklet may have been tied to my scientific bent. I adored Physics and Mathematics, and I'd always done quite well in them – so well, in fact, that by the time I was in ninth grade, I'd made up my mind to become a physicist. But every now and then, the immense satisfaction I derived from solving equations and physics problems would give way to a satisfaction of another kind. I would take refuge in a secret notebook where I recorded literary musings about poor, oppressed people. Or about the sound of water dripping from the ceiling into the container my mother would put next to our bed when it rained. Or about the rattling of the door to our mud-brick room when storm winds blew, as though some monster were standing outside in the dark and shaking it, and was sure to break it down at any moment. Or about ghosts that nested among the reeds in the ceiling, making me tremble with fear.

Dostoyevsky, photo Samuel Shimon

I wrote in response to a vague but urgent need to put things into words, to capture certain moments and release them onto paper, to express an opinion that had been cooking for a long time over a low flame and was finally ready to be "served up". It would be an opinion on the world in which I found myself living without knowing why, be it the "Why!" that I would later understand to be existential and philosophical in nature, or the "Why!" of daily life that asks: Why did I end up here in particular, in this harsh place where people view a woman as an incomplete entity for the simple reason that she is female, and especially if she comes from a poor family?

As I was getting ready to go abroad, my mother plopped down on a mat on the floor and started to cry. "I'm afraid I'll never see you again!" she burst out through her tears. Unlike my sisters, who had all accepted scholarships to study in Jordanian universities, I had turned down a similar offer so that I could study in the Soviet Union. I wanted to get a first-hand view of Socialism, justice and equality in action.

It was with pride – an adolescent pride, to be sure – that, on the form I had to fill out in applying to study abroad, I filled in the blank next to "Major" with the word "Physics". There was nothing to be proud of in such a choice so far as my mother or anybody else was concerned.

LITERARY INFLUENCES

Kafa al-Zou'bi in Moscow

"If you studied Engineering or Medicine, the time away from home would at least be justified," my mother said to me wistfully. She had good reason for her concerns, actually. Those who chose to study in the Soviet Union were forbidden to visit home until they had completed their academic degrees. Students who came back before having their diploma in hand faced the danger of being interrogated by Jordan's Secret Police and having their passports confiscated unless they agreed to cooperate with the authorities. That was one of the ways Jordanian Intelligence combated clandestine Leftist organizations working to establish Socialism and justice in the country.

I set foot in Moscow Airport in the mid-1980s, at which time Socialism had entered a phase that came to be known as Perestroika, or "restructuring." It later became apparent that this 'perestroika' was in reality nothing but a coffin in which Socialism had placed one foot. Those overseeing Perestroika were in a hurry to see the Socialist system place its other foot in the coffin so that they could pick it up with their fingertips, the way one picks up a bag of garbage, and give it a quick burial: without a funeral, roses or black ribbons, and without a tear being shed.

The first of these stormy gusts of change coincided with the end

Sergei Yesenin   Anna Akhmatova

of my year of language study in Moscow, when suddenly the glitter of my dreams wore off, and my idea of becoming a Physics researcher seemed so unrealistic as to be downright laughable. I had heard a lot of people say that there were no labs in Jordan that did Physics research. Instead, they said, there was a big rush to teach Religion and to open Qur'an memorization centres. And what they were saying was true. It wasn't yet time to cast the world I had left just a year earlier into the depths of oblivion. Now that the mist of illusion had dissipated, I could see clearly what the future would hold for me if I pursued my major in Physics: I would go back to Jordan to a job as a Physics teacher, and that would be that. I could still hear the echoes of the Friday sermons coming my way from a place now distant, and from years not long past. They rang out with vicious, hostile voices that were taking the country by storm, commanding people to rise up in support of "our mujahidin brothers" in Afghanistan in their holy war in God's defence. Meanwhile, Israel

LITERARY INFLUENCES

Alexander Pushkin   *Vladimir Mayakovsky*

Photos by Samuel Shimon

was storming Beirut and committing bloody murders there, on top of the massacres it was carrying out in occupied Palestine.

It was a time to defend God, not human beings, homelands, reason, philosophy, or the sciences – and hence, Physics, which was, and would remain for some time to come, the prisoner of curricula in which every lesson ended with verses from the Qur'an and prophetic hadiths that refuted any law of Physics that might prompt students to doubt unquestionable premises.

Following my mother's suggestion, I changed my major to Civil Engineering so that, at the very least, my time away from home would be justified, and I left Moscow to study in Leningrad (present-day St. Petersburg). Then one day during my senior year, I was drawn to a large book display in a bookstore's front window. After stopping to look at the titles, I went inside, full of trepidation. After all, apart from textbooks, I had never read a book in Russian. Without knowing why, I chose a novel by Soviet writer Valentin Rasputin

Farewell to Matyora *Valentin Rasputin*

called, *Farewell to Matyora*, the first literary work I decided to read in the Russian language. As I ventured into it, every paragraph confronted me with a plethora of unfamiliar words. Sometimes I would look them up in the dictionary, and other times I would guess their meanings from the context. Making my way slowly through the novel, I followed with fascination and pathos the story of a dying mother who resisted death in the hope of seeing one of her children return so that she could say her final farewell to him before the light in her eyes was forever extinguished. I've forgotten now how it ended. I do remember, though, that this novel was the one that opened the door for me to start reading Russian literature in its original language. Over a number of years I immersed myself in reading, beginning with the classics: Pushkin, Gogol, Chekhov, Nekrasov, Turgenev, and many others. These were followed by Dostoyevsky, the mighty philosopher with a concern to rescue Russia and reveal the souls of its tormented people. Dostoevsky would delve marvellously into psychological analysis, not only of individual characters, but of the social system as a whole. Then I began reading Soviet literature: Aitmatov, Marina Tsvetaeva, Anna Akhmatova, Yesenin, Mayakovsky, Gorky, and others. Then came Mikhail Bulgakov and Solzhenitsyn.

Now married to a fellow Jordanian, I was living in Leningrad, Russia's second largest city, and we had decided to settle there. By this time, the Soviet Union had breathed its last and the Socialist dream had collapsed. I was in daily contact with Russians, I listened to local news media, and I read the newspapers. Even so, I think it was literature itself that helped me most to understand the Russian people and their lived experience. I've always been amazed by the comprehensive way Russian literature treats life, by viewing people not as isolated entities but as products of the coalescence of all the components of their society: political, economic, cultural and social. This literature – and particularly the works of Dostoyevsky – concerned itself with deconstructing this reality. It was this concern that led Dostoyevsky to address political issues, especially in his two masterly novels *The Brothers Karamazov* and *The Devils* which – like the works of Andrei Bely [pen name of Boris Nikolaevich Bugaev], Bulgakov and others, followed by Solzhenitsyn – foretell what is to come and criticize it beforehand.

I now came and went in a city that was no longer a stranger to me. I was familiar with its people, its highways and byways. I was even raising a family there, and had a two-year-old son. In the crush of exploding chaos and crime, the collapse of government institutions, and the spread of misery as growing numbers of homeless went scraping through garbage bins in search of a bite to eat, I was making the rounds of the city in search of an Engineering job. "I'm an engineer now, Mama. But I'm unemployed!" My voice rang out inside me, but it didn't reach her.

One day, as I sat holed up in my dormitory room working on my graduation project, a knock came at the door. It was someone from my country who handed me a letter he had received from his family. It wasn't until I got to the last paragraph that I understood what had led him to show it to me: It contained news of my mother's passing. My own mother had died.

Later, I was to learn that my mother had been dying as I read Rasputin's novel *Farewell to Matyora*. I had always taken a materialist, scientific view of things, and I didn't believe in the supernatural. At that moment, however – the moment when I learned that my mother had died – I came to see in my reading of that novel a kind of telepathic summons from my mother which I had failed to perceive until after it was too late: "Come, let me see you for the last time!" And in fact, my mother had been asking people to send for me so that she could tell me goodbye. I learned this from a sister of

Kafa and the Snow

mine who, together with my other sisters, had decided not to inform me of my mother's passing for fear that it would interfere with my graduation. It was the same request that the mother in Farewell to Matyora had repeated day in and day out over the course of the novel. Had it been a mere coincidence, or a real-life summons that had been reaching me through a piece of literature? As I read it, I would be thinking about my mother, hoping fervently that she was all right, yet not daring to ask about her lest my fears be confirmed. There were times when I would break down in the face of the repeated request in the novel. Wiping away my tears, I would close the book and, feeling suffocated, go out into the street in search of a breath of air. I should have responded to the instinctive, subtle urge to believe what I couldn't see, and gone to see her. But by that time it would have been too late. Besides which, I hadn't yet got my diploma, and a visit to my home country at a time when it was under martial law would have meant losing all hope of going back to Russia again.

"It's too late." These were the same words my big sister had used. The bite of food in her hand halted halfway to her mouth when I told her I had come back to our hometown not just to visit her, but to visit our mother's grave. I hadn't dared try to do so for the entire eight years since her passing for fear that the grief pent up inside me would explode out of control, tearing me to pieces and crushing me at her graveside.

Staring blankly into space, my sister said: "The last time I went to

LITERARY INFLUENCES

St. Petersburg, photo by Samuel Shimon

visit her was three years ago. But when we buried her, we forgot to write her name on the tombstone. Nobody took care of that. Besides, people die here every day, and they rarely write their names on tombstones. The cemetery is full of them. So I couldn't even figure out which grave was hers. I was so confused!"

My mother lived a nameless life in a mud-brick house, and now she's nameless in her mud grave.

According to Milan Kundera, the "history of an art is a revenge by man against the impersonality of the history of humanity". It stands against the abstraction of philosophy. It is the invisible 'I'. It is the meaning of the unknown in Mathematics. It is the Physics of society. It is a geometrical structure. It is definite nouns, and marked graves.

I wasn't entirely aware of this when, at the age of thirty, I sat one

Covers of the Arabic and Russian editions of Layla, the Snow and Ludmila

day getting ready to write a reflection on a mud house whose outer walls would sprout grass in spring. I had bought myself a notebook and had begun stealing a few moments here or there, after my two children had gone to sleep, to write a text that had been keeping me awake, though I didn't know yet what it was or how to write it down. I felt that in order to get the message across, I needed intense solitude, a sky imprisoned in a window, a silence clamouring with echoes, and a pallor to snuff the echoes out. I sighed, wondering how a sigh could convey all this disquiet.

But in the end I started writing. At first I thought it was another one of those reflections that I would jot down on a piece of paper and be done with it. But this reflection kept going, and going. Disconcerted, with tears running down my cheeks, I tried to keep up with the flow of my thoughts as I waited for the moment when they would stop pouring out. It reminded me of the time when, many years earlier, I had poked a hole in a bag of wheat that was being stored in the corner of one of our house's two mud-brick rooms. All I wanted was to get a handful to roast and snack on while I studied. But the wheat came gushing out of the hole so fast and furiously that I couldn't get it to stop until my mother came to the rescue.

My mother and father, our two mud-brick rooms, the bookshelves covered with the wood-patterned adhesive paper, the wardrobe with the missing doors, the cold, the wind, the leaky ceiling, the evenings when cars would speed down the nearby international highway that connected Jordan and Syria, stirring up the stagnant air in the village and arousing in me a vague, inchoate longing for a distant world where justice and equality reigned – all this began pouring out of me, forming a vast ocean of pain on paper without my having the faintest idea when the flow would cease.

Not knowing what to call it exactly, I gave the resulting text to a friend of ours who was a professor of literature at Moscow University and a translator of Russian literature. When he called me a couple of days later, he admitted that he had felt awkward taking the manuscript from me, since he hadn't known how he was going to tell me later what he had been confident would be the case, namely, that what I'd written hadn't been worth his time, but that he had decided to take a look at the first page before he went to sleep. As it turned out, he told me, he hadn't slept till the following morning after reading the entire novel. He said he had thoroughly enjoyed it, and that he was thoroughly impressed.

"So, it's a novel?" I asked, genuinely surprised.

After publishing that piece – which turned out to be my first novel, entitled *A Mud Ceiling* – I started writing my second, *Layla, the Snow and Ludmila*, in which I took up the topic of Perestroika, the collapse of the Soviet Union and the political, social and cultural transformations that took place following that upheaval, in addition to the question of Arab identity with its cultural, historical and religious components, in contrast to Russian identity.

These two were followed by four other novels. Every time I begin a new novel, I try to deconstruct and rewrite this world as a way of understanding it, only to find that, as a result, it has rewritten me. I feel the need at last to answer the question my father never asked me before his death when I was thirteen years old. And the answer is: "I'm going to be a novelist, Baba."

Translated by Nancy Roberts

KAFA AL-ZOU'BI

The First Night

A CHAPTER FROM THE NOVEL
Shams Baidha' Baridah (Cold White Sun)

TRANSLATED BY ADAM TALIB

I shut the door behind me and explored the windowless room. The thick grey walls filled the space with a damp chill like silence fills a vacuum. The small window in the bathroom was the only one there was. The bathroom itself had been divided in two. At the back, there was a door that led to a toilet and the small window high up on the wall, and at the front was where my landlord had put the kitchen. There was a washing machine in there and next to it a stove with a single filthy burner. Above the stove, there was a shelf with some worn out pots and pans and beside the washing machine, a bucket.

So these were the old man's, then. The things he'd left behind, which no one came to claim. By moving in, I had become his heir. Then again, maybe the old man, who had lived and eventually suffocated to death here, had himself inherited them from the previous tenant. Who knew?

The room reminded me of my old bedroom in my father's house in the village. That one didn't have a door in the middle of it leading to another room; there was no corridor either. My bedroom did have a door, as did this one, but instead of opening out on to a narrow street with ramshackle houses, it led to a garden planted by my mother, and beyond it was the street, the sky, stars, clouds, and the sun. Every time I opened the door, it was like life was starting all over again. My bedroom was both a part of my father's house and separate from it. It was like me.

I was given that bedroom when I was sixteen. It was like a monk's cell, perfectly secluded, the ideal refuge for a solitude I had always longed for. At the time, the idea of having my own bedroom made me so giddy I got goosebumps. Being able to open and close the

Cover of Shams Baidha' Baridah

door of my own room whenever I wanted meant that I was finally free. At night, I would sit on the steps outside my bedroom and look through the trees to the faraway hills bathed in pale moonlight. I felt like I was sitting at the threshold of life itself, getting ready to jump, ready to venture past those hills on the horizon, the only thing stopping me was time's drag. Then I would go back into my bedroom and lie on the bed, staring at the spots where paint had spattered on the walls, sketch out plans for my future life in the spaces between them. In the morning, I would look at my dark, cracked reflection in the old mirror hanging on the wall, but all I could see was a bright, smiling face, because I was optimistic and confident like only young people can be and because I was stupid, too.

Back then I thought that life – my life – would take a different course, one that no one else had ever travelled, but here I was now in a windowless room, on the other side of the door from a narrow street hemmed in by sad houses. Alone, I scratch my head roughly. I haven't showered for a while. Frequent hunger and the constipation caused from eating nothing but falafel has given me haemorrhoids. I scratch my head and wonder how long I can hold out before I surrender to asphyxiation.

What happened to me? Once again, I ask the same question and once again it occurs to me that the answer lies at the start, specifically in fanciful notions that I had at the start, in the supernatural halo that I felt surrounded me at the start. It's hard to explain why, but it felt like the world was mine for the taking.

It was a bit like falling in love. Has anyone ever managed to convince someone, who has just been told by the person that they're infatuated with that they love them back, that the feelings they're feeling right now will die out sooner or later, that they'll grow bored of that person, maybe even resent them, and that one day they'll split up, that their heart will be filled with bitterness? Can anyone convince them that, even though they're absolutely certain that no one has or will ever feel the way that they feel about someone else, that their feelings are ordinary, that other people feel that way all the time, and that every day new lovers are falling into the trap of thinking their love is unique? It's far more difficult than it sounds. Prepare to hear the infatuated lover plead their case every which way: no one has ever felt this way before, this feeling is forever, it cannot wither.

Childhood is like the beginning of a love story. It's like those first few moments of passion. Try to convince the gullible young boy sitting on the doorstep, yearning for the hills in the distance – his only obstacle the sluggish pace of time – that there are disasters awaiting him, and that they will pass, and then one day he will die. He'll laugh at you. He'll think it's a joke. It's not because he can't imagine someone failing, or someone dying, it's because he can't imagine himself failing at something and he certainly can't imagine dying. Plenty of people around him have failed and died, and plenty more will fail and will die, but he was born to do great things. He may not know what they are yet, but they make him feel like he'll live forever and make him feel proud just to be who he is. I don't know what makes people so confident that they're not only different from other people, but better.

I can see myself. I was that boy, sitting on the doorstep, contemplating the hills in the distance as though I could only catch snippets of a song playing on the other side. All I managed to pick up were a few bars, but I was going to sing that song at the top of my lungs one day and it would be as though I'd always known it and the song would

A CHAPTER FROM THE NOVEL COLD WHITE SUN

never end.

That's what I used to think. But life disabused me of my fantasies very early on. All it had to do was teach Aisha the tune and she took care of the rest.

* * *

Aisha and her widowed mother used to come visit us from time to time. They didn't come to visit because my father, who was related to them, wanted them to, but because my caring mother felt sorry for them. Whenever they were getting ready to leave, my mother would suggest – only out of politeness – that they stay the night and they would always take her up on it. The next day as soon as they'd left, my father would fly into one of his rages. He would yell at my mother and swear that there would be hell to pay if she did it again or if she even so much as smiled at them when they came by the next time or invited them in.

These scenes cowed my mother, but the effect didn't last. She couldn't help herself. Sometimes when they came to visit, she would accidentally invite them to stay over and they did. One day, Aisha came over, showing off the new gold necklace her mother had bought her. It was a gold chain with a gold medallion with the word Allah written on it. It made her so happy whenever anyone commented on her necklace. She would grab the gold medallion and gush about how heavy it was and how much it had cost. She uttered the words slowly and laughed idiotically as she spoke. Her mother was wearing gold bracelets, which she'd bought for herself. She had saved up the rent she got from some land she owned and converted it into gold because she was convinced, not only that gold was a safe investment, but that it made you feel important, that you were worth something. It made them feel as worthy as the people who looked down on her daughter and herself for not having any jewellery.

They used to sit right next to my bedroom door on the stone bench that faced the kitchen on a carpet my mother rolled out for them. Aisha's mother always began by telling stories she had already told about how disgraceful people were. Someone's son got married and she and her daughter weren't invited. The same thing happened when someone held a banquet. Another person walked past their house and didn't say hello. Whenever she spied anyone in the street through the trees in our garden, she would start talking about them and wouldn't finish until she'd told us their whole life story.

When my mother disappeared into another room, they would sit there silently, impatiently waiting for the call to prayer so they could pray. If, during all this hand-wringing, a cat caught a bug or an ant carried an object larger than itself on its back or a dog outside barked causing our dog to bark back, they would both simultaneously say, "Praise be to God". They said it like they were short of breath.

Everything about the natural world was beyond their comprehension so they were constantly in awe. It didn't matter if it was something that happened in nature or in society, they always attributed everything to a higher power that controlled the world and all its crazy coincidences. It was their advanced stupidity and naivety that made me wonder why they were even alive in the first place. There didn't seem to be any difference between a world with them in it and a world without them. Was there?

That's when I started to obsess about questions I couldn't get answers to. It didn't matter how many people I asked or books I read or time I spent puzzling. Even if the ideas I developed about the universe and life and God were simple – I was trying to arrive at them without any training after all – I was certain that I was different. That there was a substantial difference between a world with me in it and one without.

Now I can at least laugh about the absurdity of someone who wonders about another person's value to the world while totally certain of their own. I used to think intelligence was what made a person's presence in the world meaningful – as though I were myself intelligent – and so I imagined that others were stupid because I thought I was better than them. But reality isn't like that at all. I can see its deeply sardonic aspect and it fills me with embarrassment.

Oh well.

Aisha and her mother stayed the night the last time they came to visit. As soon as they had left the next morning, my father erupted with anger.

"What was I supposed to do? Kick them out?" My mother pleaded.

"Yes!" He shouted back. "I'm not obliged to entertain and feed these people several times a month."

A CHAPTER FROM THE NOVEL COLD WHITE SUN

"They don't come here because they're hungry. They come here because they're lonely."

"They can go to hell! I don't ever want to see them in my house again."

What my mother said about them being lonely got stuck in my head. I imagined their little house on the outskirts of the village near a cliff-edge. On the outskirts of life near the edge of being forgotten. I couldn't get to grips with the idea that there was no cure for loneliness, and it didn't even help to be stupid and naive.

About a week after their visit, we heard the noise of screeching brakes and a forceful collision followed by screaming coming from the street outside. The sound of the brakes and the collision only lasted a few seconds at most, but the screaming carried on. I dropped the book I was reading and ran outside. People were hurrying to the scene; I was one of the first to see it. The body of a heavy woman dressed in black lying in the street at some distance from a stopped car. The driver, a young guy, was in shock. The colour had drained from his face.

The sun was behind him, heading west, shining a pale yellow light, nuzzling the shoulders of the hills in the distance. Dogs were barking loudly and, in the distance, bells chiming softly signalled that a herd of sheep was drawing near.

The driver started shouting and howling. "She came out of nowhere! I swear to God she came out of nowhere!" No one was listening to him. They were all rushing to the victim's side. It was the widow, Aisha's mother, and she had died instantly. I knew that her stillness only meant one thing: she was dead. It terrified me. That accident forced me to confront the terrifying truth: life is a delusion, a bubble. It can be popped at any moment.

The men, including my father, examined her and tried reviving her. Nothing happened. Someone said: "There's no hope."

"She could be in a coma! Only a doctor can tell," another guy shouted. My father agreed with him. He said they had to take her to the hospital no matter what because there was a procedure that had to be followed.

He began directing the men as they picked her up off the ground and moved her. That's when I saw the blood on the road and the blood pouring from her now torn headscarf. My father was shouting orders at the men who were lifting her, but not helping himself. "Pick her up from here. Your side is slouching. What's wrong with you?" They put her in the perpetrator's car and someone volunteered to drive because the driver, who wasn't from our village, was too traumatized.

I watched the whole scene in shock. I listened to the uproar and the panicking voices that transcended it. I saw the disbelief and terror in everyone's eyes. A woman screamed at her child not to cross the road, as though death were lying in wait just at the halfway point. As though death was searching each of us, looking for one more soul to steal away.

That's when I saw Aisha in the distance running towards the crowd. A little boy was running ahead of her. A group of women surrounded her and began explaining what had happened. Her eyes were as wide as saucers. I could tell the women were speaking to her as though they were talking to a young child. When she finally understood that her mother had been hit by a car, she started looking everywhere. "She was hit by a car? Then what? Where did she go? I can't see her." The words came out hesitantly.

"They took her to the hospital in town in the car that hit her."

"When is she coming back from the hospital?"

"We don't know. We want her to stay there a while, not come back quickly."

"Why don't you want her to come back quickly? I want her to come back quickly!"

The women didn't know what to say. Aisha was quite simple, so she failed to understand what they were trying to imply. One of the women took it upon herself to explain the issue as clearly as she could: "We are worried that your mother may have died, Aisha." She was waiting for Aisha to start weeping and wailing, but she didn't. She just stared at the woman in shock.

"What do you mean 'died'?"

"'Died' like died," the woman answered.

"You mean, like she died and won't be coming back because they're going to bury her?"

"Yes. She died and they're going to bury her."

Aisha finally came to face to face with her tragedy. She broke down, shouting and groaning. My mother spoke to the women: "Pray for her, ladies. She may still be alive. What's with you all? Burying her so prematurely?"

A CHAPTER FROM THE NOVEL COLD WHITE SUN

Aisha turned to look at my mother and asked her, through sobs: "You mean she's not dead? They're not going to bury her?" The other women lost it at that point. They all started crying and then they gathered around her and led her back home where they could better look after her. While all this was taking place, my mother saw me out of the corner of her eye. She came over to me, dragging my younger brother and sister by the hand so they wouldn't run off. It was as though death's shadow had descended on the village and was stalking the streets.

"You need to go back home and finish studying. You have an exam tomorrow. Also we left all the doors open." She went to catch up with the other women, but then she turned and told me not to cross the street until I was absolutely certain there were no cars coming. She begged me to be careful. My mother's deep and sincere worry moved me. It was as though everyone was a potential target now that the death of Aisha's mother had let danger loose.

I thought it was strange how everyone was so frightened of death. They were in despair, in torment, but how could you feel despair and torment about something that was the inevitable end of everything? So long as there was another life on the other side, wasn't death just something you had to pass through? If they were truly certain there was another life, they wouldn't have been so upset. Death wouldn't be so tragic. People would just say goodbye to the dead like they say goodbye to people going on a trip. It would hurt less.

I went back home and shut all the doors, then I went to my room, sat myself on the doorstep and stared into the distance. All I could think about was a word in the shape of a body lying immobile on the ground: DEATH.

I realised at some point that the sun had set. That a day had come and gone as I sat there thinking of ways to solve the problem of death. I was worried that tomorrow would dawn before I could find a way to secure my immortality.

Now that makes me laugh. Here I was in a windowless room desperately fearing the dawn because I had failed to find the tiniest shred of hope, any at all. I got up and turned off the lights so I could go to sleep. I walked through the thick darkness towards the bed and hid myself in it. The wind shook the door sporadically as though it were knocking. It slipped through the cracks and hovered in the darkness.

A CHAPTER FROM THE NOVEL COLD WHITE SUN

Then it found me. I shivered in the bed that I had brought with me from room to room: a thin mattress and a ragged blanket that were no match for the cold.

I was listening for footsteps in the racket the wind was making outside. Every time someone walked past I would listen intently to their footsteps until they faded away in the distance, leaving a void that made me feel frightened and alone.

I heard her footsteps on the pavement. The wind died down a bit and my door stopped rattling. It was like they were also eagerly following that sweet rhythm drawing nearer as if out of a dream. But when I went to the door, I saw that she wasn't alone. She had linked arms with Aisha and they were walking along like two old friends, talking and understanding each other without the slightest effort. They stood at my door. They whispered something to each other and then they stepped back. As they withdrew into the distance, their bodies became one, their faces became a single face.

I opened my eyes, startled by the horror of that thought. I didn't want to believe it was Aisha. I wouldn't believe it. It was just my mind recycling old memories. I closed my eyes.

Then, little by little, I started to hear groaning; it sounded like it was coming from the walls. There were footsteps again suddenly. They were soft, every footfall landing with care. It was as though the person was struggling to forge a path through the dark and the wind. That was when I heard her sobbing, heavy slow sobs resounding in the air like a person's last breaths. Then I heard the door handle jiggle as though someone were trying to open it.

I froze to the spot. My chaotic thoughts froze, too. My body and my mind braced themselves.

It was the old man who had died and rotted here. I was certain of it. He was trying to open the door so he could escape. As soon as I arrived at that certainty, I saw him staring back at me. Weak, suffering, miserable eyes begging for compassion. I jumped up and turned on the lights. My hands were trembling. I searched every corner of the empty room. Nothing. The old man's eyes and his footsteps had disappeared, but his panting still emanated from the walls, heavy, like someone drawing their last breath.

Fadia Faqir reviews
**Shams Baidha' Baridah (Cold White Sun)
by Kafa Al Zou'bi**
Published by Dar al-Adab, Beirut, 2018
ISBN: 9789953895567. Pbk, 318 pages
Shortlisted for the 2019 International Prize for Arabic Fiction

"Who Broke Your Wing?"

"Wretchedness unfailingly finds me," is how the main character of *Cold White Sun* begins the narrative. The room he rents had been occupied by an old man who died recently and the stench of death fills the space. The landlady interrogates him because he is a stranger. The narrator feels like fleeing, an urge that he always has. He thinks of synonyms for the word "stranger": "Absence. Aliens belong to 'some-where' not 'here'. And that 'some-where' is absent, but this 'here' is present, and its presence alienates us." This sets the tone for a dark novel preoccupied with philosophical questions about existence, religion, knowledge, mind and reason.

Rai, the protagonist, is an undervalued teacher of children who are uninterested in knowledge, and an avid reader of banned books who tops up his meagre income by writing essays for postgraduate students. The money he makes barely covers his expenses: food, rent, books and alcohol. He grew up in a small town in the south of Jordan and, when he was sixteen, he had a room of his own, a space to read, reflect, and dream.

But misery found its way to him. The feeble-minded Aisha, who, after the sudden death of her mother in a car accident moves in with them, offers him her body and he gives in and accepts her offer with open arms, even though she is mentally challenged and unaware of the complexity and gravity of the situation. "I gave in again to a visit in the middle of the night when the eye of my conscience was closed. And Aisha thinks that the act is not under His eye." Her pregnancy out of wedlock marks the end of his feeling of superiority over his corrupt father. He begins to question himself: is he her victim? Is she his victim? Or are they both victims of the customs and value system of their society? Their liaison has tragic repercussions: his father beats Aisha to abort the foetus, kills it in the womb, and Aisha dies. The narrator is convinced that he had killed her. This episode turns him from a teenager full of hope and romantic ideas to a lonely man unable to acquit himself.

His self-loathing begins as he travels from the small village in the south to the capital Amman and then to Zarqa, where he meets Ahmad in a bar, and they become friends. Unlike Rai, Ahmad is a "normal" civil servant, who has a wife, children and a steady job. Also, Ahmad, who is always dressed in a suit, believes in the capitalist system, so he keeps borrowing money, investing it, then losing it. Slowly the challenges Ahmad is facing become clearer to Rai, the image of the perfect family slips and reveals a disappointing picture. His wife keeps leaving him and going to stay with her family in Amman because of the cruelty of his mother. This conflict between his family and his wife makes his life miserable, especially because he is in love with her. As for the capitalist system, it promises so much and delivers very little. Due to his unwise investments, Ahmad cannot make ends meet so he gets an extra job in a grocery store, where he arranges vegetables and sells them. In a moving scene Rai comes face to face with Ahmad at the grocery store and watches him doing a menial and humiliating job. Yet Ahmad's love for his wife sustains him and helps continue his struggle to provide for her and his children, though because of the cruelty of his mother she decides to leave again.

Early on, Ahmad introduces Rai to Mazin, a survivor and mercenary, at the same time a believer and nonbeliever who prays with his boss and drinks with his friends. He argues that capitalism is evil but condemns strikes. Mazin is a liar, skilled at navigating a path for himself, which leads to his own happiness and gratification. He encourages Rai to satisfy his sexual urges by using a cheap prostitute. After one of their visits, Rai is astonished at Mazin's lack of empathy towards the woman's sad children as they watch cartoons and listen to the banging of their mother's bed against the wall. Mazin is offended by Rai's questioning, which goes against his strategy in life, namely avoiding meaningful questions and turning a blind eye to the injustice and misery around him.

Ahmad assures Mazin that he is happy, that his wife has returned and he will be reunited with her soon. When they both travel with their families to celebrate Eid, Ahmad commits suicide, slaughtering himself with the same knife his father was about to use to kill a lamb in an "obedience ritual" carried out by Muslims at Eid Al-Adha. The Festival of the Sacrifice, as it is also called, centres on the story of Abraham and the great sacrifice God asked him to carry out in a dream. Ahmad decides to end his wife's misery – and his – by closing the circle and taking his own life.

Years later, Rai meet's Ahmad's wife in a public library and falls in love with her. Love could have been a consolation but, ridden with guilt, Rai keeps accusing Ahmad's wife of killing him. His relentless questioning, doubt and inertia cost him dearly. He succeeds in driving her away and in ending a love which could have been a distraction from the absurdity of it all. Alive, passive, and unable to commit suicide, he slowly descends into madness, shouting "I killed him", referring to Ahmad and to his father.

Rai's father, who represents political and religious power, is a key figure in the narrative. "Our house appeared in the distance, bleak and miserable, not only because of its structure, but because it belongs to my father. Its walls reflect his anger and yelling, especially when he sees me reading. He is convinced that books distracted me from what is important in life; worshipping God and searching for means to accumulate wealth." His father wants him to be "normal" and to "resemble others".

The incident with Aisha reveals how corrupt and hypocritical Rai's father is. Religion for him is just a set of rituals, devoid of any moral or ethical meaning or implications. Islamic Shari'a law stipulates that the wealth of orphans is not to be confiscated and that they must be sponsored. Aisha was an orphan, and Rai's father took her in not as an act of kindness, but to get his hands on all her wealth. He confiscated her gold jewellery, was keen to get compensation from the driver who ran over her mother, took power of attorney over her and was keen to control her house and inheritance. Yet he worries about how much food she eats, and even the amount of soap she uses when she has a shower. To avoid spending anything on her he plans to marry her off, he would then enjoy her wealth.

Belief in destiny, the divine and the unknown goes against rational thinking. Stark and complex realities needed to be examined, problems addressed, and solutions found, but society is in paralysis because of its belief in the supernatural, in fatalism and in an unquestioning acceptance of God's trials and tribulations. The main character has no illusions about his surroundings and sees reality as it is, without a shred of romanticism, which puts him in direct conflict with his father and other so-called believers.

Like any despot, his father's enemy is education and he believes that the books his son reads have turned him into a heretic, an infidel and a loser. He threatens to burn them. Rai sees books as the only solace in his lonely existence. He spends most of his money buying them, storing them in boxes and sneaking them from one place to another to ensure their safety. When his father catches him reading *Naqd al-Fikr ad-Dini (Critique of Religious Thought)*, a book that questions dogma and encourages rational thinking and science, he becomes angry and decides to burn Rai's books. But when Rai convinces him he could sell them for a handsome price, he does not carry out his threat. His father "knows the price of everything and the value of nothing" and, therefore, the conflict between Rai and his father intensifies. The books are personified as runaways chased from one hiding place to another. Rai hides them with an Egyptian migrant worker, with a woman bartender, then with a grocer. He is fleeing, and his books are fleeing with him, all are fugitives from a society that does not value knowledge. "Panting, I run carrying a box full of books, looking for a safe haven among the short grass, among the long grass." When his father finally succeeds in finding the books and burns them, Rai vows to kill him. But one of his problems is his inertia. Like many intellectuals in the Arab world, he is good at diagnosing problems, posing questions, looking for answers, but when he finds them, he never acts or follows through. As a result, Arab societies are in stagnation and are still at the stage of magic – with an irrational belief in witchcraft and in the supernatural – rather than the stage of science – with logic, rationality and belief in the tangible and measurable. Rai, who is plagued by self-loathing, fear and a sense of looming doom is passive, and therefore his corrupt, hypocritical father comes out victorious in their "war", which happens to be fought in Jordan.

Similar to classical Russian literature, place is significant and acts as one of the characters in this novel. The novel starts with: "The village has submitted its fate to God, praised Him for His trials and the tribunals of His worshippers." Constrained by its belief in the supernatural, and controlled by imams, or those who pretend to be pious to advance their agenda, the village is unable to progress.

Place is also used as a metaphor for the different stages of the narrative and for the main character's development and state of mind. The reader can see how the trajectory of space moves slowly from freedom to confinement. As a teenager, Rai was still a romantic who sees the world through rose-tinted glasses. Back then, his room overlooked a world that seemed limitless: "a yard, which my mother planted and turned into a garden, and a street, sky, clouds, stars and sun". The world was full of possibilities until the tragic incident with Aisha changed it all. Now the room becomes smaller, overlooks a wall and some waste pipes, where an old man had died and his decomposed body later discovered. Rai lives in this room accompanied by the spectre of the old man, a constant reminder of his own immortality and inevitable death. Then he lives in a room without windows, then in a mental hospital.

Al-Zou'bi presents the village, Amman and Zarqa as desolate spaces full of, at best, inactive, fatalist people and, at worst, corrupt hypocrites. Jordan's landscape is bleak, wretched and gloomy, which matches the hopelessness and absurdity of Rai's life.

The novel establishes an intertextual relationship with other texts, mainly *The Epic of Gilgamesh*, which is quoted a few times, and Albert Camus' *The Myth of Sisyphus*. Gilgamesh, the king of Uruk, sets out to look for the secret of immortality. He befriends Enkidu, a free spirit who lives with animals – grazing at their meadows and drinking at their watering places. At first glance you assume that Ahmad is Enkidu and Rai is Gilgamesh, the tragic figure who represents man's striving for glory and immortality, but the main character's name Rai, which is rarely used, means "shepherd" and his character is injected with traits attributed to Enkidu, such as his free spirit and his pursuit of greener pastures. In a skilful reversal, Gilgamesh's lines are given to Ahmad, who knew the way and realised that happiness and immortality are unachievable and, therefore, committed suicide. Al-Zou'bi injects each character with traits that belong to both Gilgamesh and Enkidu. When Ahmad commits suicide both Gilgamesh and Enkidu do too, which emphasises the darkness of her narrative and her insistence that death triumphs at the end. Humbaba wins, and the snake's eternal youth is renewed and guaranteed. What remains for Rai between his birth and death is a sense of confinement and a severe existential crisis.

Philosophical questions punctuate the narrative, and are raised in every scene – while the main character is doing household chores, teaching, walking, having a drink or talking to friends. Rai lives without meaning and sees suicide as a way out but is too weak to commit it. Al-Zou'bi quotes the playwright, moralist and political theorist Albert Camus' *The Myth of Sisyphus*, highlighting the relationship between her novel and Camus' analysis of nihilism and the nature of the absurd. The narrative cannot be understood or possibly enjoyed without knowledge of the works of philosophers like Søren Kierkegaard, Arthur Schopenhauer and Friedrich Nietzsche, who argue that life is essentially meaningless although humans continue to try to impose order on it and look for answers to unanswerable questions.

Camus uses the Greek legend of Sisyphus, who is condemned for eternity by the gods to repeatedly roll a boulder up a hill only to have it roll down again once he gets it to the top, a metaphor for the individual's persistent struggle against the essential absurdity of life. Rai is Sisyphus, who continues to roll the boulder up the hill although he realises that the act is meaningless. Ways out of this confinement are either death or suicide and both are unavailable to Rai, who is ridden with shame and self-loathing doubt and is totally passive. The only outcome is his descent into madness, when all his flashbacks, his gloomy present, philosophical questions, and the women he had known become jumbled up in his mind. Faces and histories merge, which probably hints at the deeper truth that we are all one and the same person, Sisyphus, Gilgamesh, Enkidu, Rai, Ahmad, and Mazin, are all doomed and prisoners of this existence with no way out. Both our nights and days are dark and without hope.

Echoing Fyodor Dostoevsky's *White Night*, which is told by a narrator suffering from loneliness and is divided into night and day, *Cold*

White Sun has fourteen chapters that alternate between night and day. The final two nights and days are not numbered and show Rai's descent into madness. It seamlessly shifts between past and present, where the present frames and defines the past and vice versa. Their relationship is polemical.

Al-Zou'bi uses stream of consciousness, interior monologue and intertextuality to create a multi-layered, modernist novel with traces of post-modernity, where the social realism of great Russian literature is mixed with absurdism and existential philosophy. The narrative is dotted with incidents created to put philosophical questions to the test, such as: are we essentially good or bad? And what is this existential war we are all engaged in? Was it imposed on us? Are we victims or perpetrators? With an inferior narrative and less skilful pen, this angst and repetitive raising of existential questions might irritate readers, but the beauty of the stripped and bleak narrative and the continuous attempts for redemption sustain our interest.

Some sections, although stripped back and austere, rise to the level of poetic prose. In this extract Rai is having coffee with Ahmad's widow: "Although she didn't talk to me about Ahmad, he was present. Present in the midday heat, in the scent of the flowers blossoming next to us, in the roar of the traffic, in the creeping footsteps of passers-by, in Fairuz's voice singing 'They went to graze their sheep, and the grass is right here on my ribs'. A wild, silent cry in the heart of everything around us, giving it a sad rhythm, similar to rain darkening our thoughts as we watch it through a glass window."

This rich, multi-layered tapestry exposes both external and internal conflicts, where both the individual and the society he lives in are disintegrating. Corruption and decay are widespread. There is something rotten at the heart of the Arab world, and this novel shines a cold white sun on it to objectively and dispassionately diagnose its malaise. It is a triumph and deserves to be put on the shelf with great Arabic fiction, where it will sit comfortably.

GUEST WRITER
LINDA FRANCE

In 2018, Linda France was the first UK writer to take part in Alta'ir, an artistic exchange with Jordan, initiated by novelist Fadia Faqir, with New Writing North and Durham Book Festival. For the month of September, she stayed with the Council for British Research in the Levant in Amman and the work presented here arose from her first impressions of Jordan gleaned on that visit. *Banipal* invited Linda to be the Guest Writer of this issue.

Linda has published eight poetry collections (with Bloodaxe, Smokestack and Arc) and several pamphlets, often in collaboration with visual artists. *The Gentleness of the Very Tall* (Bloodaxe 1994), a Poetry Book Society Recommendation, was longlisted for the Los Angeles Times Book Prize. *The Toast of the Kit-Cat Club* (Bloodaxe 2005) is a verse biography of the 18th century traveller Lady Mary Wortley Montagu. Her latest collection *Reading the Flowers* (Arc 2016) reflects Linda's increasing interest in ecological themes and was written during a Grand Tour of thirteen of the world's Botanic Gardens. It also contains her poem 'Bernard and Cerinthe', winner of the Poetry Society's National Poetry Competition in 2013. Her anthology *Sixty Women Poets* (Bloodaxe 1993), a PBS Special Recommendation, hailed as 'ground-breaking', went into four editions.

Since the 1990s, Linda's work has taken her to many countries for residencies, fellowships and research.

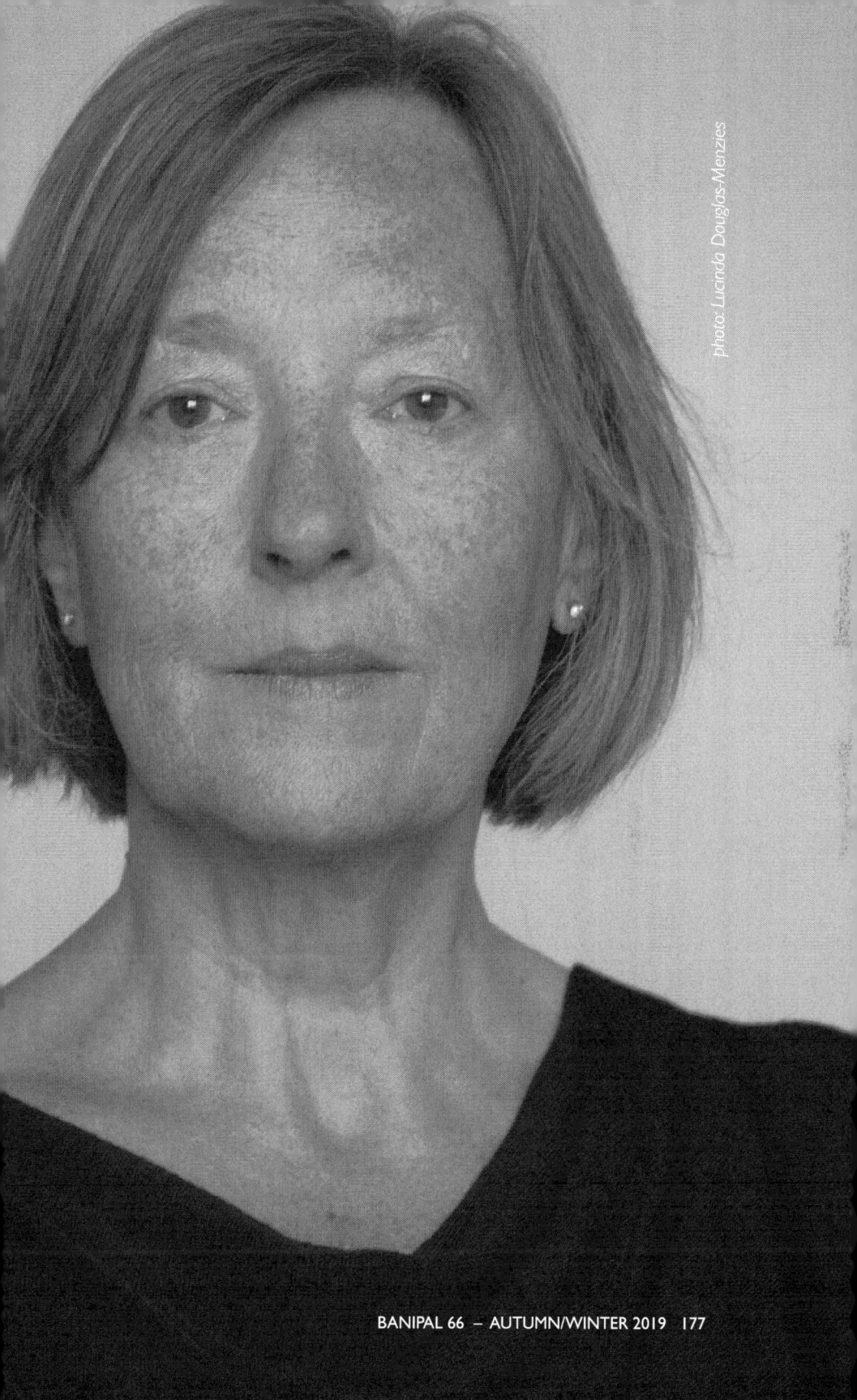

LINDA FRANCE

Four Poems

WILD PISTACHIOS

When any of us step outside our front doors we can usually be guaranteed to find what we would expect to find, to see what we are in the habit of seeing. In my case, the view that greets me is acres of arable land, sometimes with, sometimes without, sheep or cattle. I have the measure of this place, and perhaps it of me. I know where I fit within its slow-to-change rural ecology. Travelling to a new country – indeed a new continent – with a different front door and for-a-time-unimaginable view is a step into the unknown. Nothing can be taken for granted. You are given the chance to be reborn, to come wet into the world again, eyes screwed up against dazzling light, assailed by sounds you don't know the source of. Everything will demand a response – fight or flight. Surprise is good medicine for a writer, hungry for fresh impressions, illuminating perspectives on our troubled, tangled world.

Gertrude Bell knew this when she began her exploration through Syria in 1905, which she wrote about so evocatively in *The Desert and the Sown*:

To those bred under an elaborate social order few such moments of exhilaration can come as that which stands at the threshold of wild travel. The gates of the enclosed garden are thrown open, the chain at the entrance of the sanctuary is lowered; with a wary glance to right and left you step forth, and behold! the immeasurable world. The world of adventure and of enterprise, dark with hurrying storms, glittering in raw sunlight, an unanswered question and an unanswerable doubt hidden in the fold of every hill. Into it you must go alone, separated from the troops of friends that walk the rose alleys, stripped of the purple and fine linen that impede the fighting arm, roofless, defenceless, without possessions. The voice of the wind shall be heard instead of the voices of counsellors, the touch of the rain and the prick of the frost shall be spurs sharper than any praise or blame, and necessity shall speak with an authority unknown to that borrowed wisdom which men obey or discard at will. So you leave the sheltered close, and, like the man in the fairy story, you feel the bands break that were riveted about your heart as you enter the path that stretches across the rounded shoulder of the earth.

Even leaving my house, stepping out of my front door at 3.30 in the morning, I saw my own field afresh – the night sky bright with stars, the Plough scooping me up all the way to Newcastle airport for my early flight to Paris, the first leg of my journey. The unknown had already begun to scatter its dark magic.

Before my trip, I'd had several conversations with people who knew Jordan and had also done some reading but I was aware I couldn't quite penetrate the membrane of the words used to describe the country. It felt like the façade of a frontier town – all apparently in order but with no third dimension, no depth, certainly nowhere for me to live, however temporarily.

"My Jordan", the country so far existing only in my imagination, was all wild pistachios, pomegranates and figs – a simulacrum of the enclosed garden in the Song of Solomon – what I hoped was a peaceful, safe and fertile place, albeit surrounded by countries at conflict with themselves and each other. Turning my destination into a garden, perhaps especially a Biblical one, was an early attempt at translation, trying to build a bridge between known and unknown worlds. I really had no idea. I was nervous of Orientalism, worrying about making my garden too exotic. Even the phrase 'Middle East' is a moot point – whose middle? A few years ago visiting Australia, I was humbled to discover that what we call the Far East is their Near North. The Levant although it sounds old-fashioned, is perhaps a preferable term – coming as it does from the French *lever* – referring to the place where the sun rises.

Travelling all through the day and arriving in the dark is not unlike being blindfolded, spun round, somewhere you don't know, having the blindfold stripped off and being told to find your way home. As the plane came into land, I could see Queen Alia airport, all lit up, rising and falling, its wavy roof designed to evoke Bedouin tents in the desert. Then, at nearly midnight, I was acutely aware I was being driven in a car by a man I'd never met before who spoke no English, on the right hand side of a three-lane highway, past enormous signs in a script I couldn't read, to arrive at a street in a city with nothing in it that I recognised. I climbed out of the taxi and promptly fell off the pavement, not anticipating it to be nearly two feet above the road. Why would I? My brain was half asleep and my legs didn't know where they were.

Linda France during her residency in Jordan

I punched in the key code on the gate, then another on the side door and, on my third attempt, open sesame. Everyone in the building seemed to be in their beds – which was where I was heading, even though none of it made sense – not the marble floors, the timed light switches, the disconcertingly mirrored lift reflecting back a women surely much older than me, my room on the top floor (F5) hot and strange, incomprehensible plugs, a fan I couldn't make work however many buttons I pressed…However, horizontality was what I wanted more than anything else in the entire world and within ten minutes of crossing the threshold, I lost consciousness. Until around 4.30, when I was woken by the sound of a man's voice, the muezzin's call to prayer – "Allahu akbar . . . God is the greatest . . . Hasten to the prayer . . . Prayer is better than sleep." Infidel, I turned over and fell back to sleep. I'd forgotten to put any mosques in my garden.

Later in my stay, I wrote a note to myself – *Where is the poetry here?* A big question, practically deafening. I did find some wild pistachios – one tree was nearly 500 years old, gnarled bark split and fruits attacked by a gall. Some of the younger healthier varieties I came across had fruit within reach. They were nothing like any pistachios I'd ever tasted – the tiny pink berries were sharp in my mouth, acid with tannin – briefly refreshing on a hot day, but neither sweet nor delicious. They were unexpected, entirely original. Like Jordan, they were what they were – incontrovertible, distinctive, tantalising. I knew almost as soon as I tasted them that in 'my Jordan' they had the power of Persephone's pomegranate seeds – and even only eating a few meant that I would have to go back. The country and its fruits had got under my skin and I'd have no choice but to return and keep pushing beyond the limits of everything I didn't know about the world and myself. *Where is the poetry here?* Only *everywhere* – as long as you are attentive enough to hear it and you're ready, like Gertrude Bell before you, to feel the *bands break that were riveted about your heart as you enter the path that stretches across the rounded shoulder of the earth.*

LINDA FRANCE

WOMAN AS A FLOWER CALLED AUTUMN

Observe what I have become –
a thin white raceme rising
from a fat papery bulb.

Call me khareef, autumn –
squill, pollinated by wind,
wasp, hornet or bee.

My inflorescence, a plume
of hardly there: oldest flowers
at the base, new ones bloom

as my shoot grows, white on white
on white. Ancient tincture,
kill or cure, I ward off rats,

NEXT ISSUE

POEMS BY TWO WINNERS OF MOROCCO'S ARGANA INTERNATIONAL POETRY AWARD

LEBANESE POET
WADIH SA'ADEH, 2018

TUAREG POET
HAWAD, 2017

evil. This the dry
has taught me — how much asks
to be sacrificed, the boon

of everything stripped back,

bones of autumn blossoming.

Amman, September 2018

DESERT PIANO

The square tread of your Toyota Cruiser
cracked open the flint's first chinks as we drove,
insinuating as the wide palette

of stones, sun glare squinting off every curve
(chipped and smooth) — gunmetal, black, charred ochre:
earth's utterances arcane, particular

as fallen stars, orphan wishes still locked in.
Outside, from magician's hands, you let fly
two padded runnels for flat rocks gathered

like children in your arms. Struck with globed wands,
notes rang out, vibrating through the flint, us;
our bodies back-lit with stark melody

and rhythm, hearts beating to the spheres' tunes,
in an upturned bowl of dark desert,
a morning's drive beyond the city's lost

stridencies. You tracked the pitch of each note
on your phone — a yellow, blue, green sequence,
landscape DNA. In my small fists, beaters

carried the music's silica current
up my arms, on fire, diamonding muscle
and bone — a snake of sound, tongue-tied, scale-skin

chert: billion-year old language with no words
the badia was singing, if we'd only listen.
Whatever it was – trance or haunting,

some djinn? – it took root inside me: a vow
of unsilence; love's sharpness, the pitch
and play of incalculable stones.

For Ammar Khamash
On the way to Qasr Tubah, September 2018

CALLIGRAPHY, AMMAN

Everything I do these days is a poem
about not having enough time. I want
to write them down – all those stories I brought home
inside me, like the women who, with a prayer, sew
a sprinkling of earth from their villages
into the black hems of their dresses
to carry with them wherever they go.

I'll write from right to left
so I'll always know where I've been, remember
what I've lost, what I've left unfinished:
a library of stone my children can pick over
when I've gone. Isn't there always more dust to sift,
for me and for them, more seeds, sumac
and sesame, to sow? The living is the lasting poem.

And I must write it over and over –
like the wild scatter of crocuses
blooming in the desert, palest mauve, gold
with pollen. No water for miles. Inshallah,
there's still chance to circle and return,
more lines to find. Let me be that eagle I saw,
beak and quill, inscribed on the sky's blue door.

BOOK REVIEWS

Hassan Abdulrazzak reviews
Sentence to Hope: A Sa'dallah Wannous Reader
Translated from the Arabic and with an introduction by Robert Myers and Nada Saab.
Published by Yale University Press (The Margellos World Republic of Letters), March 2019.
ISBN: 978-0300221343. Hbk, 464 pages, USD38.00 / £25.00. Kindle: USD30.72 / £21.38

The Shakespeare of the Arab World

I was talking to the Lebanese writer and performer Hanane Hajjali earlier this year, at a reception held by the biennial Shubbak Festival in London of contemporary Arab culture, about Manara Theatre, the new theatre company I have formed with playwright Hannah Khalil and actor/producer Taghrid Choucair-Vizoso. I was telling Hanane that one of the aims of the company was to put on readings of 'classic' Arab plays. Hanane's eyes brightened. "You have to do the plays of Sa'dallah Wannous. He is the Shakespeare of the Arab world," she said.

This might seem like a bold claim but the comparison is perhaps far less hyperbolic than one first imagines. Both writers created fables, drawn from folkloric stories or history, to shed light on political and social themes. Both writers were operating under systems of censorship. Yet Wannous remains virtually unknown in the English-speaking world. Indeed Marvin Carson, The Sidney E. Cohn Distinguished Professor of Theatre, Comparative Literature and Middle Eastern Studies at City University of New York, has described Wannous as "one of the major undiscovered treasures of world literature". Until recently his plays and writing were unavailable in English. *Sen-*

tence to Hope is the first major survey of Wannous's work, containing not only translations of four of his major plays but also a selection of articles and interviews that illuminate the work.

Wannous was born in the village of Husayn al-Baher in northern western Syria in 1941. He grew up watching farmers enact impromptu dramas full of black humour and listened to folkloric stories and poetry, all of which later influenced his work. In 1966, Wannous moved to Paris to study theatre at the Sorbonne and that's where he ended up writing his first major play after a catastrophic event took place.

In June 1967, Israel defeated in six days the combined Arab armies of Egypt, Jordan and Syria, gaining control of Jerusalem, the West Bank, Gaza, the Sinai, and driving some 100,000 Syrians from their homes in the Golan Heights. In his essay "The Dream Falls Apart", included in the book, Wannous describes how this catastrophe forced him to ask: "Why do we write? . . . that question made me feel as if I were swallowing a handful of razor blades . . . words were defeated and language had collapsed." He dropped a project he was working on and began to write *An Evening's Entertainment for the Fifth of June*. The play was influenced by the work of Bertolt Brecht (amongst others) who sought to erase the fourth wall between the audience and the stage. In the stage directions, it is indicated that the play should start later than scheduled. Actors sitting amongst the audience begin to complain about the delay. Finally the director of the theatre appears on stage and apologizes to the audience that the play they were going to perform was cancelled due to a fallout with the playwright "Abdalghani". The latter joins the director on stage and the two begin to bicker, to the dismay of the audience. We get snippets of their play, which turns the Six-Day War into a story of valiant soldiers and heroic village men who massacre their women so that they are free to resist the Israelis without fear of being disgraced by having their womenfolk raped by the invading army. Abdalghani, however, realises his play is no good.

BOOK REVIEWS

Sa'dallah Wannous (1941–1997). Banipal No 1, February 1998, paid tribute to the revolutionary playwright, who had died the previous May, in a heart-felt and compassionate article by Peter Clark "Remembering Sa'dallah Wannous".

BOOK REVIEWS

Sa'dallah Wannous (left), in a humorous moment, congratulating Egyptian actor Salah al-Saadani (centre), who had played the title role in his play The King is the King

Abdalghani: My words *(he shakes his head and raises his voice)* – I smelled them as they lay on the lines of the pages. They had a smell that reminded me of the vaginas of prostitutes. I may be wrong. Other people can't perceive the smell of these words and use them now just as they did before, without suspicion or unease.

The director, having given up on putting on a show about heroism, instead gets dancers to perform traditional folklore as a way for the audience to experience "happiness and nostalgia", but his plans are scuppered when villagers wander onto the stage and begin to tell what actually happened during the war as opposed to the mythologised play the director was trying to put on. Towards the end of the play, armed men appear and a mysterious "Man in a Suit" makes a lengthy speech, blaming the dissent of the audience on imperialist interference before rounding up some of the spectators, who manage to make a call to arms before their arrest.

The play ran for two nights in Damascus in 1968. Wannous was terribly disappointed by its reception. "I felt a renewed sense of bitterness the evening of every performance," he wrote in "The Dream Falls Apart", "people would applaud and then leave the theatre as they always had . . . The audience did not erupt in demonstration." To a modern reader this seems like a hopelessly naïve expectation but one has to remember that Wannous was only 26 when he wrote this highly ambitious play.

Wannous drew inspiration from *The Thousand and One Nights* and historical chronicles. This was evident in *The Adventure of the Head of Mamlouk Jabir*. The play opens in a café where the men are waiting for the *hakawati* (a traditional storyteller) to arrive and entertain them. They are hoping that he would tell them an epic of victory and glory to cheer them up but the *hakawati* instead tells them the story of the slave (mamlouk) Jabir who takes advantage of a feud between the Caliph and his Vizier by offering to act as a messenger to the Vizier, his master, so that he could deliver a letter to King Munkatim, the Caliph's enemy, to invade Baghdad. To improve his prospects in the court, Jabir comes up with the plan that his head could be shaved and the message written on it. This plan not only draws admiration from the desperate Vizier but also from the café customers watching this play-within-a play and commenting on it. They admire Jabir's ambition but as events unfold, they discover that the Vizier had written on Jabir's skull an order to have him beheaded once the message is read. Wannous instructs that the same actors play the Vizier, the Caliph, King Munkatim and their respective subordinates to highlight the interchangeability of the various ruling elite. Jabir wants to get rich quickly and marry his beloved Zumurrud but he ends up paying the ultimate price for his haste. The play makes the audience question the price of going along with a corrupt regime.

When president Anwar Sadat spoke at the Israeli Knesset in 1977, a year before signing the Camp David Accords, Wannous saw this, as the translators wrote in their introduction, as "a complete capitulation to a colonial oppressor and a US proxy". Towards the very end of his life, Wannous was interviewed by his friend the filmmaker Omar Amiralay in a documentary entitled *There are Many Things Still to Say* (1997). Wannous describes the intense depression he felt as a result of Sadat's capitulation, where even the rays of the sun entering his room felt like a foreign invader. He wrote that day a text entitled: "I'm the coffin and the mourners together." He took an overdose of sleeping pills and was in a coma for several days. He stopped writing plays for over a decade after that.

In 1990 he was diagnosed with cancer. The sense of imminent death spurred him on to write seven new plays in the last years of his life. Amongst them are two plays included in this volume: *Wretched Dreams* and *Rituals of Signs and Transformations*. What immediately distinguished these plays is that at their centre are fully imagined female characters seeking emancipation. In an interview included in the book, Wannous describes how he let go of his self-censorship of only writing about what he felt were "important causes" and writing began to feel like a "pleasure". In *Wretched Dreams*, Ghada and Mary are trapped in miserable marriages. Their lives are briefly brightened by the arrival of a lodger, Bashir, a man Mary thinks could be her son and who reminds Ghada of her brother. Bashir brings hope into their lives. When he is evicted, they conspire to poison their husbands in order to gain their freedom with tragic consequences reminiscent of Greek dramas. Dreams and reality collide in this delicate play that perfectly demonstrates how the personal and political are intertwined.

The last play in *Sentence to Hope* is *Rituals of Signs and Transformations*, a play considered by many to be Wannous's masterpiece. Set in the 19th century and inspired by true events, the play begins with Abdullah, a Naqib (a member of the notable elite of the city), having a licentious evening with Warda (meaning flower), a prostitute. They are arrested by the police chief, who hopes that Abdullah's humiliation will please his rival the Mufti (top Islamic jurist). But the Mufti is alarmed by the potential scandal. "Whoever acts towards the Naqib with such disrespect may do so with the Mufti at a moment's notice," he says. The Mufti devises a plan whereby he would sneak into the prison Mumina (meaning believer), the wife of Abdullah, so that she can take the place of Warda and everyone can pretend that an innocent misunderstanding took place. Mumina reluctantly agrees to the plan on the condition that the Mufti promises her a divorce from her husband. It is at this point that the characters begin to transform. Mumina decides to become a prostitute for real, renaming herself Almasa (the Diamond) and becomes Damascus' most notorious courtesan. Abdullah renounces the worldly pleasures he previously enjoyed and becomes a Sufi ascetic. His journey has echoes of Shakespeare's King Lear. The Mufti is transformed by his desire for Almasa.

Mufti: I don't know if it's temptation or madness. From the moment I met you, your image has been following me. You've troubled my spirit and perturbed my heart. I don't know what to say. Please be reasonable and accept my offer.
Almasa: Is it love, our Mufti?

Mufti: I don't know what it is. Don't ask me. Do you accept my proposal of marriage or not?

Almasa: Our paths are different and my desires can not be satisfied by marriage.

In seeking to liberate her body and soul, Almasa sets in motion a very different kind of revolution than the one envisioned in *An Evening's Entertainment,* Wannous's first play. People are not thinking of taking up arms to liberate themselves in *Rituals* but instead are seeking personal liberation in a hypocritical society. Wannous seems to have come to the realisation that women's liberation is not a marginal issue, to be dealt with once the entire society gains freedom, but is in fact at the heart of the struggle for equality and democracy. The theme of the play is perhaps best articulated in a subplot where the homosexual strongman Al-Afsa comes out by shaving off his moustache and giving it to his lover, who ends up rejecting him. Al-Afsa reflects: "If you suppress and conceal, you live well . . . if you're true to yourself . . . you become an outcast." *Rituals* doesn't give easy answers. Every character who attempts to liberate him or herself pays a price be it their sanity, social status or even their life.

Sentence to Hope is a landmark publication that will hopefully bring Wannous the attention he richly deserves in the English-speaking world. The translation is extremely accurate and the different registers of Wannous's language are admirably captured. Very occasionally it lapses into the literal as when one character in *Rituals* says "as everyone knows my hand is extended" when he means he is generous. Minor changes will probably be needed depending on where productions will take place but this translation provides a solid foundation to build upon.

As the Western world slides further into the arms of populist and/or authoritarian, right-wing regimes, it could benefit greatly from hearing the voice of an intellectual who spent his life struggling against repressions of all kind. Wannous's work could not be more urgent today.

In "Thirst for Dialogue", a speech he gave to mark UNESCO World Theatre Day, Wannous said: "Theatre is more than simply an art. It is a complex cultural phenomenon without which the world would become lonelier, uglier and poorer . . . We are sentenced to hope."

BOOK REVIEWS

Susannah Tarbush reviews
The Fetishists: The Tuareg Epic by Ibrahim al-Koni

Translated by William M Hutchins
University of Texas Press (Series: CMES, Modern Middle East Literatures in Translation), 2018
ISBN: 9781477317891. Pbk, 568 pages, $30.00 / £23.99. Kindle: $7.96/ £22.79

Savouring the taste of life

In his author's note to the translation of this monumental work, the Libyan Tuareg novelist Ibrahim al-Koni recounts the extraordinary real-life incident that inspired the novel. His older brother had bet another man that whoever succeeded in scaling a certain tall cliff face in the Tadrart mountain range in Libya would win one hundred camels. "That person actually won the bet; once he reached the top of the cliff, though, he could not climb back down and perished on the crag. He won a hundred camels, but lost his life."

Al-Koni cites the New Testament: "For what will it profit a man, if he gains the whole world and forfeits his life?" (Matthew 16:26). These lines are also the epigraph to the chapter "The Wager" in *The Fetishists*. The New Testament reference is typical of the wide literary and philosophical and religious allusions which occur throughout the novel.

In *The Fetishists* it is the love of two rivals for the Sultan of Timbuktu's daughter Princess Tenere that leads to a wager. She has been unable to choose between the two suitors: "Her freedom led to her falling in love with Okha's nobility, grandeur, and dedication to ceremony at the same time that she loved Udad's heart and fondness

for singing and the mountains."

An intermediary conveys the wager from Okha to Udad: "If you can climb up Idinen and stand on its top vertical slab, he will relinquish the princess." Udad accepts the bet. His name means Barbary ram, and he is known for his climbing skills. But Idinen will be difficult to ascend. Referred to by the Tuaregs as "the Mountain of the Unknown and the Jinn", it is reputed to be both haunted and sacred

A crowd gathers to watch Udad start his long ascent. Al-Koni gives a thrilling, minutely detailed account of the days Udad spends climbing. We enter his thoughts and reflections as he ponders the mysterious Tifinagh lettering and paintings left by ancestors on the walls of caves, and sees visions of the sacred Barbary ram Amghar.

Al-Koni's writing is transcendental and mystical: Udad embraces the slab and "his senses dissolved into the slab's senses, melted into the rock's arms, united with the beloved, with the celestial, supernatural stone. As he approached paradise, intoxication spread through his organs. This inebriation pervaded him. He had never experienced or savoured such euphoria before." But after he starts to think about Tenere things change: "the rock had rejected him the moment a woman entered his heart". There is celebration among the people below when they know he has reached the summit. "The jinni has climbed to the land of the jinn." But Udad's success leads to Okha's self-initiated destruction. As for Udad, he now faces a perilous descent.

Al-Koni was born in 1948 near the Libyan city of Ghadames and was brought up in the tradition of the Tuareg, learning to read and write Arabic at 12. He studied comparative literature at the Gorky Institute and then worked as a journalist in Moscow and Warsaw. He has lived in Switzerland since 1993.

His writing is deeply rooted in his Tuareg background. An astonishingly prolific author, he had by 2007 written more than 80 books – novels, short stories, poems and aphorisms – and received numerous awards. His works are translated into some 35 languages and he was in 2015 a finalist for the Man Booker International Prize, a sign of his global stature.

A steady stream of English translations of al-Koni's work has appeared this century. And yet it is only now that *al-Majus* has appeared in English, in William M Hutchins's translation, despite the fact that it is regarded as his masterpiece. The German translation by Hartmut Fähndrich *Die Magier – Das Epos der Tuareg* (Lenos Verlag) appeared as long ago as 2002, and Philippe Vigreux's French translation *Les Mages* (Editions Phébus) was published in 2005. The appearance of *The Fetishists* in English fills a long-felt gap.

The French and German titles are close to the Arabic original, *al-Majus*. So why is the English version entitled *The Fetishists*? In his translator's note Hutchins explains that al-Majus "literally means the Magi or Magicians, in other words, the Zoroastrians . . . From a Muslim point of view, and especially from a Sufi one, Zoroastrians are the Other". In al-Koni's novel, however, the Other is not the Zoroastrians but adherents of traditional West African folk religions. "The Bambara and other Bantu characters in *al-Majus* are the Other – both because they are polytheists or 'animists' (rather than monotheists) and because they practice settled agriculture." Since the term *al-Majus* is used pejoratively in the novel, it has been translated as "Fetishists".

"Fetishist" also has a second, neo-Marxist use related to Marx's discussion of "commodity fetishism". In his French translation of *al-Majus*, Philippe Vigreux says Al-Koni has explained that "al-Majus" denotes both African Fetishists and anyone who substitutes a cult of gold for worship of God. Commodity fetishism could also extend to petroleum – "black gold".

Taboos over fetishism and the use of gold are a recurring theme in *The Fetishists*. Towards the end of the novel, after the destruction of the splendid new city of Waw, the diviner Idikran strangles the Sultan of Waw, Tenere's uncle Anay. "You didn't realize that gold dust destroys a fortress," says the diviner. "No creature who has adopted it for a god escapes destruction. You overlooked the fact, poor wretch,

BOOK REVIEWS

Ibrahim al-Koni

as many before you have, that anyone who believes in gold dust and worships it blasphemes against monotheism and the Holy Quran. Sultan of Gold Dust, which of us is the true Fetishist?"

Anay was estranged from his brother Oragh the Sultan of Timbuktu. He built Waw as a rival to Timbuktu which had long been the gold capital. The concept of Waw recurs in al-Koni's works: it is the lost oasis, a paradise, of the Tuareg people.

Oragh's status in Timbuktu has been weakened by the Fetishist Bambara. The Bambara paramount chief plans to choose a high-bred virgin to present as a human sacrifice to the Fetishist god of the winds, Amnay. Terrified that Tenere will be the sacrifice, Oragh sends her to safety in the Azjer area where "there are tribes that have not been tempted by the Fetishists' gods".

The opening pages of *The Fetishists* depict the first encounter, by chance, between Udad and Princes Tenere. Udad has been up in the mountains: the novel's first sentence is: "Anyone who has not breathed mountain air will never savor the taste of life." Tenere has just arrived in the area with the caravan transporting her to safety. The first chapter is entitled "The Qibli Wind". The Qibli is the south wind from the desert, and is a quasi-character in the novel.

Al-Koni has a tremendous gift for description and his poetic prose, dazzlingly translated by William Hutchins, is mesmerising. *The Fetishists* is vast in scope, covering more than 550 pages, and has a complex structure with multiple storylines and a narrative that is organised in a non-chronological fashion. Reading it is a totally immersive experience, and is aided by an invaluable guide in the appendix to 53 of the novel's characters, and a glossary of around 150 terms from Tuareg culture, history, religion and geography.

The book consists of two volumes, written over the course a year

from December 1989. Each volume is divided into two parts, and there are in all 27 chapters, each preceded an epigraph. The epigraphs come from a variety of sources reflecting al-Koni's erudition and wide reading: they include the Old and New Testaments, the Qur'an, Herodotus, Tuareg legends, classical Arab authors, Erich Fromm, Thomas Mann, Claude Lévi-Strauss, *The Book of the Dead* and August Toschi's *Ornithology of Libya*.

Hutchins has over the years built up a reputation as one of the most prolific and respected of Arabic literary translators. He was joint winner of the 2013 Saif Ghobash Banipal Prize for Arabic Literary Translation, for his translation of *A Land Without Jasmine* (Garnet Publishing, 2012) by Yemeni author Wajdi al-Ahdal. His translation of *The Fetishists* is currently among the 16 titles entered for the 2019 prize.

The writer-translator relationship between al-Koni and Hutchins has borne much fruit. Hutchins won the National Translation Award (NTA) in 2015 for his "stunning" translation of al-Koni's novel *The New Waw; Saharan Oasis* (The Center for Middle Eastern Studies at the University of Texas at Austin, 2014). The NTA is awarded annually by American Literary Translators Association (ALTA).

The New Waw is the first title in al-Koni's Oasis Trilogy, and The Center for Middle Eastern Studies at the University of Texas at Austin also published Hutchins's translations of the other two books in the trilogy: *The Puppet* (2010) and *The Scarecrow* (2015). In addition, Hutchins has translated al-Koni's *The Seven Veils of Seth* (Garnet Publishing, 2008) and *Anubis* (The American University in Cairo Press, 2014).

Banipal has reviewed translations of several of al-Koni's novels. *Anubis* was reviewed in *Banipal 23*, Summer 2005, *Bleeding of the Stone* (Arris Books, 2004), translated by May Jayyusi and Christopher Tingley), in *Banipal 19*, Spring 2004, and *Gold Dust* (Arabia Books, 2008), translated by Elliott Colla, in issue 33, Autumn/Winter 2008.

The epigraph at the beginning of *The Fetishists* is from Goethe's *From my Life: Poetry and Truth:* "Every nation, if it wants any prestige, must possess an epic, though not necessarily in the form of an epic poem." Al-Koni has certainly succeeded in writing a magnificent Tuareg epic in *The Fetishists*, and one that a reader is likely to return to again and again.

Stephanie Petit reviews

**Printed in Beirut
by Jabbour Douaihy**

Translated by Paula Haydar
Published by Interlink Publishing,
August 2019.
ISBN: 9781623719906. Pbk, 220 pages,
$15.00

Smoke and Mirrors

Jabbour Douaihy (b. Zgharta, 1949) is arguably best known in the anglophone world for *June Rain*, his powerful novel based around a 1957 massacre in the Lebanese village of Burj al-Hawa. The book was shortlisted for the inaugural International Prize for Arabic Fiction in 2008, and published in an admired English translation by Paula Haydar in 2014, that was the "highly commended runner-up" in the Saif Ghobash Banipal Prize for Arabic Literary Translation that year. His novel *The American Quarter*, longlisted for the IPAF in 2015, was published in translation, also by Paula Haydar, in 2017. The novel under review, *Printed in Beirut*, his third translated by Haydar, is a coltish, lighthearted novel that follows the scandalous affairs of an old Beirut printing press.

The story begins with Farid Abu Shaar, a budding young author who, having just completed his first novel, traipses from publisher to publisher in the hope of finding someone who will recognise its unparalleled genius – "I squeezed the juice of my being into this book!" he exclaims at one point. But, as one publisher scolds, "no one reads", the age of book printing is over, and his manuscript is rejected by them all. Abu Shaar's last stop is 'Karam Brothers Press, Est. 1908', a huge outfit that prints seemingly everything, from books about indigenous Mexican cultures to shopping bags stamped with designer logos. Predictably, its owner too has no interest in Abu Shaar's novel but, as the company has just lost its Arabic language copy editor, he offers Abu Shaar the position. Humiliated but with

BOOK REVIEWS

Jabbour Douaihy

few other prospects in sight, Abu Shaar accepts, and spends his days proofreading instruction manuals, directions and descriptions of "the treatment of haemorrhoids using bee honey". His literary pursuits crumble under the crushing mundanity of the task. The lone handwritten copy of his novel adorns his desk like a sad memento of his erstwhile lyricism. Then, one evening (and rather inexplicably) his most treasured possession goes missing and, around it, an intricate web of secret liaisons, criminality and duplicity is revealed. The manuscript (or, rather, a beautified version of it) appears in the publishing house's office several months later, exquisitely typeset in *thuluth* calligraphy, and printed on paper that is "thick and difficult to bend, as if wax-coated". The mastermind behind its resurfacing, it emerges, is Persephone, who, lonely in her marriage to Abu Shaar's boss, develops an infatuation with the dreamy young author. Moreover, business is very good at Karam Brothers – suspiciously good, in fact. Indeed, ever since Karam Brothers Press acquired its Heidelberg Speedmaster XL 162, "the most advanced digital press in the Middle East", well, it is like they're printing money. And of course they are – on the same paper used in Abu Shaar's book. When an international police operation locates the source of the counterfeit euros in the Beirut printing press, Abu Shaar's book is confiscated by the authorities, and the unfortunate author finds himself caught up in a large-scale investigation into the press's century-long trail of forgery and fraud.

Weaving back and forth in time, space, and between characters, *Printed in Beirut* is a spirited and lively little novel. But, unfortunately, Douaihy's distinct rejection of a clear linearity in favour of multitudinous diversions weakens the narrative, and the story is frustratingly lacking in focus. A tighter reworking, one feels, could have brought out the smoke-and-mirrors intrigue surrounding the printing press more successfully. As it stands, *Printed in Beirut* brims with ideas, but is pulled in too many directions.

As a lighthearted comedy of errors, however, there is much to be enjoyed. It is packed with a host of engaging (albeit cartoonishly exaggerated) characters. Abu Shaar especially is a recognisable exemplar of the kind of protagonist common to the genre: hapless and confused, buffeted by events rather than the instigator of them. His otherworldliness sets him apart in the cut-throat contemporary publishing industry. His earnest faith in his literary talent is the butt of the novel's running joke. Unsurprisingly, for the work of an author whose artistry is so clearly enmeshed in the stories of his homeland, *Printed in Beirut* also conveys a strong sense of place, and makes ample use of the city's mosaic of cultures and sects. Karam Brothers Press, employing "Maronites, Orthodox, Armenians, Sunnis, and Shiites", reads as a kind of microcosm of Lebanese society, while the novel's tracing of the press's multiple reincarnations responds to, and runs in parallel with, the country's tumultuous recent history.

Once more, kudos must be awarded to Paula Haydar for her skilful translation. Indeed, in the finer moments of *Printed in Beirut*, Douaihy incorporates beautifully a variety of references to classical Arabic literature, as well as richly detailed passages about printing machines and typeface blocks. In Haydar's translation (and aided by welcome endnotes) these are a wonderful asset to the book, and provide an affectionate ode to a craft that is fast disappearing.

Elias Khoury
The Novelist

Special feature
Banipal 67, Spring 2020

Hannah Somerville reviews
The Clothesline Swing by Ahmad Danny Ramadan
Published by The Indigo Press, UK, May 2019. ISBN: 9781999683368. Pbk, 220 pages, £12.99 / Kindle: £6.02
US Edition by Nightwood Editions, California, May 2017 ISBN: 978-0889713321. Pbk, 288 pages, $21.95.

Places of solace

On occasion, the role of fiction is not merely to demonstrate the scope of human imagination but also where it necessarily comes to an end. Ahmad Danny Ramadan's award-winning, lyrical debut, *The Clothesline Swing,* first published in the US by Nightwood Editions in 2017, and now brought to readers on the other side of the Atlantic by new independent publisher The Indigo Press, issues forth as a cry of resistance from the ontological shoreline: a love letter to people and places penned from the very edge of a world fast becoming inconceivable. From its arresting frame story, in which a first-person narrator named only as Hakawati (storyteller) tells his terminally sick lover tales to keep him alive through the night, bursts forth a proliferation of anecdotes that clatter backwards and forwards in time, seamlessly blending the quotidian with the mythic, and memory with history, traversing half the globe from Damascus to Cairo to Wreck Beach, Vancouver. But we know, and Hakawati knows too, that all of this is only buying time. "I'm saddened to realize," he reflects in a moment of circumspection, "that even if I am imagining this world around me, my imagination limits me to an ending where you, my dear, will die."

In a poignant reworking of the Scheherazade fable we are introduced to a Syrian man and his lover, now old and living out their twilight years in Vancouver. The pair, we learn, fled Damascus in 2012 and alighted in Beirut before travelling to Canada in a saga that

mirrors Ramadan's real-world journey as a refugee. Decades later, Hakawati tells his listless beloved a story – or three – every night, to keep him from slipping into oblivion: raging, unilaterally, against the dying of the light.

The author himself is a Syrian-Canadian and dedicated LBGTQ-refugee activist. At just 35 years old Ramadan writes with rare skill and singular intimacy that draws the reader inextricably into the lives of his two ageing protagonists and holds them there, captivated. Amid the clutter and squabbles of day-to-day living and the creaks and sighs of the old house, Ramadan elicits a clear sense of embattled, enduring love between the two. They are not wholly alone, though: a jocular personified Death now also roams the house, smoking hash in the living room, eavesdropping and making acid remarks about the "lunatics" who enlisted him decades to harvest a million Syrian souls – and occasionally conjuring up the ghosts of the past.

The stories Hakawati recites to his lover are suffused with both poetry and painful reality, by turns fantastical and rooted in bitter, lived experience. The couple's tentative early encounters in civil war-torn Damascus are nostalgic but startlingly bereft of cliché: "I roamed the corners of your body," he remembers, "like a lost traveller exploring the old sleepy streets of the city, knocking on the doors of your soul with the tips of my fingers like a shy delivery boy knocking on the wooden doors of old homes in Sarouja carrying warm bread and baladi cheese."

Other episodes are presented in elegant triptych form, including three tales of Syrians at sea, and three symbolic accounts of the long trajectories of Beirut, Cairo and Damascus, reconfigured in Hakawati's fevered imagination as mermaids. There are stories of camaraderie and subversion: a raucous group of friends throw back

BOOK REVIEWS

Ahmad Danny Ramadan

shots and play Mortal Kombat while bombs extinguish the lights of old Damascus and individuals are "disappeared" at random by the *mukhabarat*. There are also innumerable tragedies. "My nose is filled with the smell of my burned memories," Hakawati reports, recalling a nightmarish scene in which his unstable mother sets fire to their family photographs. In a moment of near-magical realism, this protagonist, immobilised by grief, eventually vanishes from the world altogether. Each interpersonal exchange in *The Clothesline Swing* is rendered all the more potent by the knowledge that at any moment, one party or another may disappear.

Romantic relationships in Ramadan's novel are presented in a refreshingly optimistic light, almost uniformly tinged with discovery and mutual understanding. But they are also fragile, and homophobic violence ravages Hakawati's stories, from a vicious attack outside a cinema in Cairo to his first love's forced marriage, suicide and burial in a rain-soaked, unmarked grave. On the former, the narrator reports being "skinned" of his innocent earlier self and split into two people: flayed alive by socio-political circumstance, just as uprooted Syrians the world over have been forcibly divested of their former lives. The narrator recalls the pain in his lover's eyes at his maltreatment in Beirut, while Ramadan uses their 'fictional' journey to highlight often-overlooked aspects of the refugee experience. There is a bitter diatribe on the politics of terminology such as "displaced persons", and the couple are thoughtlessly "tokenized" in New York by a friend who refers to them as "his refugees". There is also the pain of watching one's homeland being obliterated from afar. In one devastating passage, Syria herself is re-imagined as "a glass ballerina" smashed into a thousand blood-tipped shards: "Her head, removed by the fall, stares at me, asking me to fix her. Her arms, dismembered from her body, are hopelessly waiting on the floor."

The theme that resonates the most intensely across Ramadan's novel, though, is that of hope and survival – and of the discrete places in which its protagonists find solace together in an otherwise unforgiving world. The title refers to a makeshift swing set up in the narrator's early family home, bedecked with jasmine flowers and recalled in the rose-tinted manner of a fairy tale. Though the swing does not last, the escapism it represents does. "You hold my hand closer to your body in bed and I slide my body next to yours," Hakawati says to his lover. "We look each other in the eyes for a second. We smile. We sleep. In my dreams, we live happily ever after."

The tales he weaves, borne out of love, lend dignity to their predicament and allow both to imagine a better world. And *The Clothesline Swing* achieves the same. Out of the ashes of calamity, Ahmad Danny Ramadan has created something immeasurably beautiful.

BOOK REVIEWS

Becky Harrison reviews
**The Book of Collateral Damage
by Sinan Antoon**
Translated by Jonathan Wright
Yale University Press (The Margellos World Republic of Letters), May 2019.
ISBN: 9780300228946. Hbk, 312 pages, $24.00 / £16.99.
Kindle $20.18.00 / £16.14

The umbilical cord of loss

Translated by Jonathan Wright, *The Book of Collateral Damage* is the fourth novel of Iraqi novelist, poet and translator Sinan Antoon. Loosely based on his own experiences of revisiting Baghdad in 2003 to make a documentary, it is his first set in the United States, where he has lived on leaving Iraq in 1991 after the beginning of the Gulf War. It is easy to see much of Antoon's life in the US in that of the main protagonist Nameer, who is a PhD candidate and literary translator also living in the States for over a decade. This blurring of fiction and reality is an important theme of the novel, and makes for an interesting negotiation between the reader and the author.

We are introduced to Nameer in a hotel in Baghdad in 2003, where he has travelled as a translator for an American documentary. It is his final day and, between seeing family, he encounters an enigmatic bookseller called Wadood on al-Mutanabi Street, a road famed for its second-hand booksellers and a natural draw for bibliophiles. After an initially frosty start, Wadood tells Nameer about a documentation project he's been working on, "the project of a lifetime". He shows him a neatly arranged file of written notes, clippings and photographs, and explains that it is "an archive of the losses from war and

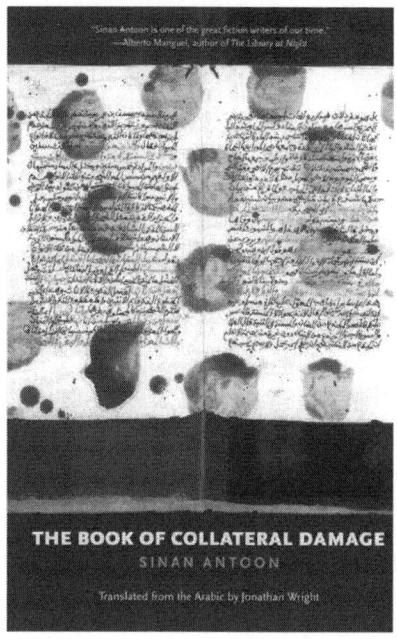

destruction" – a catalogue or index of "anything that can be destroyed. Minute by minute." One minute occupies an entire folder.

Documentation in the face of destruction is at the heart of *The Book of Collateral Damage*, and it is this interaction between Wadood and Nameer that is the catalyst for the story. We learn that, after an initial refusal to share his work, Wadood entrusted Nameer with the first chapter of his catalogue, which he delivered to his hotel in Baghdad along with a letter promising to keep in touch. Their connection is born, and with it, the driving force of the novel, as the reader follows Nameer back to his uneasy place in the diaspora, where he begins to explore and translate Wadood's catalogue and becomes increasingly obsessed with his own documentation.

The jarring experience of being an Iraqi "behind enemy lines" is a key theme which Antoon handles with an expert hand, peppering Nameer's first-person perspective with microaggressions from all sides: new colleagues immediately ask him about the war in "his country", or whether he is Shia or Sunni, while state officials refuse to grant him a driving license without a birth certificate because an "Arab like him' tried to cross the border. Even in Iraq, acquaintances confront him about his allegiances and family questions whether he remembers the streets of his youth. The muted, repetitive tone with which Nameer reports his daily life and the frustrating interactions that dominate it portray a depression before it is ever named by the character. With few friends nearby, a string of failed relationships, and a reluctance to finish his dissertation, during the first half of the book Nameer's character is defined by his failure to connect with or be understood by those around him, despite having made the US his home for over a decade. In one memorable moment, a student taking

Sinan Antoon

his Arabic language class – a condition of the job, as opposed to his academic specialism – takes him by surprise by enquiring how to say "Kneel down. Stop. Put your hands up. Move back" in Arabic. The student explains that after graduating he will be joining the army and going to Iraq or Afghanistan, "where these phrases will be essential". Shocked, Nameer refuses to tell him the phrases or even write them down.

The structure likewise alludes to the push and pull of feeling away from home, jumping from present, to past, and between Wadood and Nameer's writings, separated only by a fraction of indentation. Within the two men's first-person perspectives, Antoon deftly interweaves myriad other sources, from Walter Benjamin quotes, to letters, dreams, poetry, and lists. The most striking of these intermissions are the "colloquies" which form the unusual recording style of Wadood's catalogue. These, also first-person, tales of creation, life, and death, are scattered throughout the novel, catapulting the reader into the life of a foetus, a kashan rug, a prize racehorse, or a child talking about his friend's stamp collection. As Wadood said in his explanation of the catalogue to Nameer in their first interaction, his focus is on "the losses that are never mentioned or seen", the things which seemingly disappear into an abstract nothingness: the black hole of collateral damage, rarely reported or noticed by the outside world.

Over the course of the novel, the shifting of perspective intensifies, and the lines between the two men become more blurred as each excavate their pasts and their respective traumas through their writing. The novel's success lies within this sense of confusion, and with its abstract, often cosmic, exploration of war and the mental, physical, and metaphysical destruction it wreaks. Nameer asks "Is this incessant desire to archive everything a sickness?" but, if anything, Antoon offers the documentations of Wadood and Nameer as a cure, as a means to connect a destroyed world to the living, and the living to one another.

In the most striking colloquy of all, Wadood's catalogue describes its task of documenting the losses of each minute of the war: "It is exactly the opposite of the task of the midwife or the obstetrician who cuts the umbilical cord after the birth. I reattach the umbilical cords between things and their mothers . . . It's tiring work that never ends." This could be the voice of Antoon himself, whose novels continue to connect readers to his homeland.

BOOK REVIEWS

Clare Roberts reviews
**Celestial Bodies
by Jokha Alharthi**
translated by Marilyn Booth
Sandstone Press, UK, 2018
ISBN: 978-1912240166.
Pbk, 256 pages, £8.99 / $18.00
Kindle: £3.79 / $4.68
Audible audiobook $16.22

Intriguing relationships in this Omani family saga

Celestial Bodies, the title chosen for Marilyn Booth's English translation of *Sayyidat al-Qamar* (literally 'Ladies of the Moon'), shines a spotlight on Omani society with nuanced and sophisticated flare. The novel serves as a colourful history of modern Oman, told through the eyes of a cast of mainly female characters over multiple generations in the fictional village of Al-Awafi. Ambitiously, it explores the country's complicated relationship with slavery, with which – having only been abolished in 1970 – it appears to still be coming to terms. Also touched on are the Jebel Akhdar rebellion, which tore the country apart in the 1950s, and somewhat stoic memories of Oman's history as a British protectorate. Reaching up to the present day, it captures a country undergoing a period of rapid change: tradition and modernity intersect as jeeps, planes and Bedouin caravans are confronted with one another, village-dwellers move to Muscat or abroad, and women fight with their husbands for permission to give birth in modern hospitals. The novel offers an intimate narrative of the process of modernisation and its effects on the social landscape of this small country; the result is really rather interesting.

Celestial Bodies is in many respects conventional in its family-oriented themes. Lacking a page-turning plot, the reader is instead en-

couraged to piece together fragments of overlapping stories offered by different narrators. What the novel lacks in suspense, it makes up for with its fascinating host of characters who, all with their own wholly unique voices and styles, burst through the courtyards of their family homes, all holding their own secrets and questions close to their chests. At first glance, the novel centres around three sisters Mayya, Asma and Khawla, and Mayya's controversially-named daughter London. Beyond this, however, the novel spans four generations, exploring the relationships of families in Al-Awafi across time, the ties between wealthy families and their former slaves, the unrequited love of Mayya's husband Abdallah for his wife, and an illicit relationship between the three girls' father Azzan and a Bedouin woman. It offers vivid portraits of its female characters, through the naivety of the young sisters, the raw pain felt at the birth and premature loss of children, to the cool and level-headed decision of one of the women to divorce her husband over a decade into a loveless marriage. But despite the importance given to the novel's female characters as suggested by the novel's Arabic title and much of the coverage the book has been receiving, it is arguably some of the male characters that prove most intriguing. The insecurities of Mayya's husband Abdallah, for example, and the loudness of the voices in his head that never let him forget his troubled relationship with his father or his wife's indifference to him, haunt the reader long after putting the book down.

The Man Booker prize money will be shared between Alharthi and Booth, further cementing this successful author-translator relationship harking back to Alharthi's time studying for a PhD at Edinburgh University, where Booth formerly held the position of Professor of Arabic and Islamic Studies. It was during this time that Booth read

BOOK REVIEWS

Jokha al-Harthi

the Arabic manuscript of the novel, which left such an impression on her that she took the risky decision to take a chance on translating *Sayyidat al-Qamar* even before finding a publisher. The respect in which she holds the work is evident throughout her translation, demonstrated not least by the way she preserves snippets of Arabic in transliteration, which is something of a trademark of her translation work. When I asked her about her work, she told me: "I don't want the reader to have to resort to a glossary, and I don't like footnotes, so I work very hard to clue the reader in on meanings of Arabic words or phrases within the text, but without interrupting the voice." These Arabic fragments are for the most part incorporated seamlessly into the English text of *Celestial Bodies*: readers of the English come away with a deeper appreciation of the richness (and sometimes rhyme) of the original language, as well as a better understanding of the culture. Booth's translation also handles the multitude of voices, moods and time periods to which they belong, deftly: 'Getting the voices of different characters, their distinctiveness, is a translational challenge that I relish' she told me. "The array of voices (the *loudness* of voices) was certainly a feature of this novel and a challenge." Booth has navigated this challenge masterfully, capturing each character's unique style, from the rebellious hysteria of the young rebel London, to the booming crassness of former slave Zarifa, to the crippling insecurities of Abdallah. Several welcome editorial decisions have made the novel's host of characters easier to keep track of in the English translation: a family tree has been provided, as well as chapter titles indicating who is narrating each new section.

Seeping into nearly every page of this prose work is Alharthi's thorough grounding in the Arabic poetic tradition. A charming game between Asma and her father involves the two of them taking turns to recite poetry by heart in "playful competition". At other times, Azzan recites verses to his somewhat nonplussed Bedouin lover. Such moments offer glimpses into verses from some of the key poets in the classical Arabic poetic corpus, from Imru' al-Qays through to al-Buhturi and al-Mutanabbi, all translated admirably by Booth. The novel also offers an interesting introduction to the little-known Omani poet Abu Muslim al-Bahlani, a contemporary of Ahmed Shawqi. For Booth's part, she admits that she benefited from the fact that Alharthi, a scholar of pre-modern Arabic poetry from a family of poets, was on hand to assist with this. But even Booth herself appears somewhat bemused by the enormity of the task she has set herself of late, telling me: "At one point, I asked myself: What star was I born under, that three of the most recent novels I translated all had passages from the great poet al-Mutanabbi that I had to break my head against?"

In her translation, Booth has brought alive and captured the many styles and spirits of the myriad of characters that come together in this novel, as well as the idiosyncrasies of the Omani culture that Alharthi has captured so magically in her sensitive and original work. In case more evidence was needed for the fact that this translator-author relationship is one that works, Booth also plans to translate Jokha's next novel, *Bitter Orange*.

BOOK REVIEWS

Shadi Rohana reviews
Palestine +100
edited by Basma Ghalayini
Stories from a century
after the Nakba
Comma Press, Manchester, UK, 2019
ISBN: 9781910974445. Pbk, £9.99.
Kindle USD7.47

The future of Palestinian literature

In a televised interview shortly before his death, Mahmoud Darwish was asked by journalist and diplomat Nabil Amr to speak about his Palestinian literary antecedents: Who were the Palestinian poets in whose tradition Darwish inscribed? Our poet's answer was simple: "Nobody." Following a brief moment of silence and giggling among the audience in the studio, Darwish clarified that there are, actually, two ways to answer that question: the first is to give a personal answer – the answer he just stated: he did not consider his poems to belong to a literary tradition that is particularly Palestinian, while the second one is to answer in his capacity as "Palestine's National Poet" – a responsibility that had been bestowed upon him during his early poetic days. As a National Poet, the invention of a genealogy of national poets to which one belongs to becomes a duty; "only" as a poet, Darwish's literary ancestors are the poets he actually read and internalized: a handful of Arab poets from Syria and Iraq, none of which were Palestinian.

Darwish's answer invites to us to think about the open question of what really constitutes Palestinian literature today and what it might look like in the future, as well as about the book we have between our hands: *Palestine +100*, edited by Basma Ghalayini and published this year by Comma Press in Manchester (the UK).

BOOK REVIEWS

This book, the second of what is possibly a "+100" series (following *Iraq +100*, published in 2016), consists of 12 on-demand short stories: Twelve Palestinian writers were posed with the question of what Palestine might look like in 2048, 100 years after the Nakba?

We already observed the importance of the Arabic language for Darwish. Moreover, from his answer to Amr one could assume that it was difficult for Darwish to imagine himself writing in another language besides Arabic; his tradition – whether invented or recognized – belongs to the larger Arabic-speaking world, and "Palestinian literature" is literature written in Arabic by those who happen to be Palestinian.

For the editor of *Palestine +100*, however, Palestinian literature (specifically fiction prose) is not written exclusively in Arabic: only half of the stories in the book were written in Arabic and appear in English translation, while the other half appear in their English origin.

What do these stories all have in common? For the writers summoned for *Palestine +100*, the future of their country in a 100 years does not look bright: Palestine is not liberated, refugees are still refugees, Gaza remains under attack and siege, and our current anxieties are brought to the maximum:

In "N" (written in Arabic by Majd Kayyal, translated by Thoraya El-Rayyes), "The Association" (Samir El-Youssef, trans. Raph Cormack) and "Song of the Birds" (Saleem Haddad), for example, the forgetfulness of the Israeli occupation and genocide in Gaza is a reality. In the first two stories, forgetfulness is decreed by a defeatist permanent Peace Agreement signed by the official Palestinian leadership and the Israelis, while in "Song of the Birds" the forgetfulness imposed on the Palestinians is not of their past but of their present situation, and the mere awareness of the fact their country is still occupied becomes an act of resistance against normalization and the occupier.

In Selma Dabbagh's "Sleep it Off, Dr Schott" excessive religiosity leads to the creation of a secular scientific enclave in the Gaza Strip, while in Ahmed Masoud's "Application 39," Palestinian internal political division has led, along the years, to further fragmentations and the creation of what the narrator optimistically calls Palestinian "republics" (Republic of Nablus, Republic of Gaza, etc) – all of which still use the Israeli currency (the Shekel) and have varying degrees of resisting or collaboration with the Israeli occupation of their lands.

In "Vengeance," by Tasnim Abutabikh, the global ecological and humanitarian crisis led Israel to extend its occupation to the air Palestinians breath, rationing it in accordance with the "criminal record" of Palestinian individuals.

In other words, the anxiety some of these Palestinian writers express is that which has accompanied Palestinians since the Nakba: the temporal becoming permanent. Before the Oslo Accords, it was the fear that the temporal state of internal and external refuge and exile might become a permanent one; today, it is the condition of forgetfulness Palestine lives: that Palestinians, one day, might forget that they are being occupied by a foreign power they are ought to be resisting directly in order to achieve their liberation. This anxiety might partly explain why many of the writers in this collection have resorted to science fiction when thinking about their country's future.

While Palestinian reality in 2048 does not look bright for Palestinian writers as their country will continue to suffer from the Israeli occupation and further fragmentation, *Palestine +100* invites the reader to think about what new directions Palestinian literature is taking toward 2048?

"N," written in Arabic by Majd Kayyal from Haifa, employs a variety of narrative voices in different sections of the story, a technique which distances current Arabic prose from the canonical writers of Palestinian literature that are mentioned in book's introduction. While each short story or novel by writers like Ghassan Kanafani or Jabra Ibrahim Jabra had usually maintained a single narrative voice from beginning to end (or, when different narrative voices appear, they are intended to complement the story being told), the narrative voices in "N" are different streams of voices forming an apparently improvised chorus (like in Roberto Bolaño's *The Savage Detectives*).

In addition, the intertextuality and references "N" contains include foreign and Palestinian films, as well as "inside jokes" that are specific to the Arab Palestinian society in Haifa. This aspect of "N" is very intriguing, as it indicates that the growing intersection of Arabic literature with other literatures today (whether through translation or direct reading in foreign languages) does not prevent the local and common references and sensibilities of the Arab lives today from entering world literature and recovering their universal value.

This is not the case, however, of all the stories that compile this collection. Some of the stories that include Israelis as their protagonists (with the exception of Dabbagh's "Sleep it Off, Dr Schott"), for example, rather than attempting to engage with the nuances of the Israeli state from within wind up with trivializing Israeli society, and consequently trivializing Palestinians and the nature of the conflict. Such is the case, for example, of "Final Warning" by Talal Abu Shawish (trans. Mohamed Ghaleiny), where a group of Palestinians from the occupied city of Ramallah and Israelis from Modi'in —an Israeli settlement built on confiscated Palestinian land— are equally requested, by a voice from outer space in Hebrew and Arabic, to "cut it out" and cease their hostilities in this "tiny sector of the planet's orbit" since they are affecting the galaxy's stability.

Between 1981 and 1993, when Mahmoud Darwish and the Syrian Kurd Saleem Barakat edited the Palestinian Arabic literary journal Al Karmel, Palestinians were a minority among collaborators to the journal, for which literary translation was essential. The journal personified the universality and contemporaneity of the Palestinian struggle through its engagement with world literature. While the introduction to *Palestine +100* refers to absence as a defining feature of Palestinian fiction, the collection also shows its fullness and its capacity to contain many languages, genres, perspectives and contradictions.

BOOKS IN BRIEF

The 18 stories in **The Quarter** by Nobel Laureate Naguib Mahfouz were brought to light by Egyptian academic Mohamed Shoair during his research on the author's works, with a note attached reading "To be published in 1994". Introduced and translated by Roger Allen, with a Foreword by Elif Shafak, the book includes Mahfouz's Nobel Prize for Literature Acceptance Speech, and tantalising reproductions of the hand-written manuscripts of four of the stories. As analysed in the introduction, the short narratives (with a few no more than two or three pages in length) have their symbolic location in the local "quarter" where all the "foibles, conflicts, relationships, triumphs and defeats" of the inhabitants can be unveiled (no pun intended). In one, a woman returns with a baby, after a year away, and every day, holding her baby, sells sweets outside a house where she used to work, aggravating Boss Uthman until he agrees to "marry her and acknowledge the baby". The protagonists, as in all Mahfouz's works, come from ordinary local life – a wife, a clothes presser, a beggar, an orphan, a madman, a servant, a language teacher, a young divorcée, a young bride, the quarter's Imam and the quarter's Head. Saqi Books, July 2019. ISBN: 978-0863563751. Hbk, 128 pages, £10.99 / $14.00 Kindle: £5.69 / $7.11.

The Old Woman And The River, by the late Kuwaiti author Ismail Fahd Ismail, weaves an unforgettable story around the author's native village of Sabiliyat, near Basra, Iraq. The idea for it was sparked by a journalist at the end of the Iran-Iraq war, wanting to know from the author why the Sabiliyat area was luscious and green while the rest of the huge Shatt Al-Arab groves of date palms were yellow, and devastated. During that war, all residents of the area were ordered to leave, and the military demanded that the entrances of all rivers leading out of the Shatt Al-Arab be blocked up. Um Qasem, with her large family evacuated to Najaf, decides she nevertheless must return home to Sabiliyat. She is accompanied by

a donkey named "Good Omen". In a powerfully empathetic way, dodging soldiers and shells, and guided by her dead husband's words in her dreams, Um Qasem greens the orchards by thwarting the dams, telling the soldiers: "It's a sin to kill the fruit of the earth." This utterly engrossing novel, shortlisted for 2017 International Prize of Arabic Fiction, is "also about hope and the possibilities of the human spirit even in the bleakest of settings", wrote the translator Sophia Vasalou, one of the prize's judges. Interlink Publishing, October 2019. ISBN: 978-1623719821. Pbk, 160 pages, $15.00.

A Map of Absence An Anthology of Palestinian Writing on the Nakba. From the Nakba of May 1948, 70 years ago, to the present

day, this anthology gathers together poetry and prose by 49 Palestinian writers about the Nakba, in the main, or before it happened. Editor Atef Alshaer relates in his introduction how for Palestine "literature has been a source of rebirth, documentation and emancipation, engaging with a burdened reality and an ongoing tragedy". There is a roll-call of well-known authors: among them Mahmoud Darwish, Fadwa Tuqan, Rashid Hussein, Muin Bseiso, Jabra Ibrahim Jabra, Emile Habibi, Ghassan Kanafani, Sahar Khalifeh, Samih al-Qassim, Liana Badr, Ibrahim Nasrallah, Samira Azzam, Salma Khadra Jayyusi, Izzudin Manasra, Yahya Yakhlif, Taha Muhammad Ali, Ghassan Zaqtan, Selma Dabbagh, Naomi Shihab Nye, Raba'i al-Madhoun, and Lisa Suhair Majaj, plus honorary Palestinian Elias Khoury, as well as younger generations of writers such as Atef Abu Saif, Ashraf Fayadh, Nathalie Handal, Adania Shibli, Fady Joudah and Najwan Darwish. A collection that at its heart recaptures absence, loss and Palestinian history through memory and testimonies about this defining act of the 20th century, the Nakba. Edited by Atef Alshaer. Saqi Books, May 2019. Pbk, 272pp, ISBN: 978-0863569906, £16.99 / $23.95. eBook: ISBN: 978-0863569951, Kindle: £7.19 / $8.94.

The Book of Disappearance is the second novel of Ibtesam Azem, a Palestinian writer and presently a senior correspondent for *Al-Araby Al-Jadeed* newspaper, based in New York. Set in today's Jaffa and Tel Aviv, Israelis wake up one morning to find that all the Palestinians have disappeared. That is the starting point for a thoroughly thought-provoking narrative about identity, history, memory and perception of place that moves back and forth between the present and 1948 Jaffa and crucially, also, between two alternating narrators, Alaa, a Palestinian cameraman whose grandmother recently died and who has written about her and her memories in a journal left behind after his disappearance, and his Israeli neighbour, Ariel, who is confounded by the disappearance and finds the journal in Alaa's flat. As Ariel takes over his erstwhile friend's flat he re-enacts, unwittingly or not at first, the 1948 occupation of "abandoned" Palestinian homes. Excerpted in *Banipal* 54 (Autumn/Winter 2015) https://www.banipal.co.uk/selections/92/316/ibtisam-azem/. Translated by Sinan Antoon. Syracuse University Press, July 2019. ISBN: 978-0815611110. Pbk, 256 pages, $19.95 / £16.50.

The Sea Cloak & Other Stories is the debut collection of Palestinian author, journalist, and women's rights campaigner Nayrouz Qarmout, translated by Perween Richards, with the title story translated by Charis Olzok. Drawing on her own experiences growing up in the Yarmouk refugee camp in Syria and of her later life in Gaza, the author vividly describes the environment and plights that families and particularly women and girls endure in Gaza while often concluding on a hopeful, positive note. Some stories are set around key dates in Palestinian history, such as Land Day, the King David Hotel bombing in 1946, the Sbarro restaurant bombing in 2001, also around the ancient port of Maioumes, contrasting life then with now. Comma Press, Aug 2019. ISBN 9781905583782. Pbk & eBook £9.99.

Modern Sudanese Poetry: An Anthology.

Adil Babikir has done a great service to world literature in creating this anthology of translated Sudanese poetry, and he stresses that it is only a "limited cross section of the colossal mass of poetry being produced in post-independence Sudan", ie. after 1 January 1956. The voices of the 31 poets are wide-ranging, and in his introduction Babikir discusses the main themes and issues confronted by the poets over the decades – identity, Arab-Africanism and Afro-Arabism, the polarisation between Arabism and Africanism, the early waves of socialist realism, anti-colonialism, Sufism with a unique African flavour, patriotism and politics, exile, plus themes that are a complex mixture of the existential and philosophical, and the agonies of civil war. Among the poets are Muhammad el-Mahdi el-Magzoub, Mohammed el-Makki Ibrahim, Taj el-Sir el-Hassan, Jayli Abdel Rahman, Mohammed el-Fayturi, Rugaia Warrag, Najlaa Osman Eltom, Nylawo Ayul and Rawda el-Haj. Translated and introduced by Adil Babikir with Foreword by Matthew Shenoda, University of Nebraska Press, African Poetry Book Series, September 2019. ISBN 978-1496215635. Pbk, 186 pages, $19.95 / £16.99. eBook (EPUB & PDF) $19.95 / £16.14.

Incomprehensible Lesson is a selection of poems by the late Iraqi poet Fawzi Karim, in versions by Anthony Howell, who worked from the author's own versions. They explore the poet's experience of becoming at home in London, passing from a sense of exile to a sense of uneasy belonging, starting with a return to the beginnings of literature in Iraq – the "Epic of Gilgamesh". Fawzi Karim, who died in May this year and had lived in the UK since 1978, was born in Baghdad in 1945. This is his 2nd selection of works in versions by Anthony Howell, following *The Plague Lands and Other Poems* (2011). Carcanet Press, January 2019. ISBN: 978-1784104283. Pbk, 96 pages, £9.99 / $14.99. Also available as eBook (kindle, & PDF).

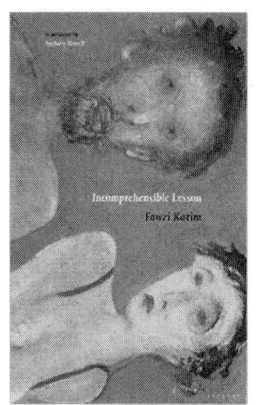

BOOKS IN BRIEF

Bitter English by Ahmad Almallah is the poet's first collection, which he wrote in English, and in which he lives through his experience of being a Palestinian immigrant and newly becoming an American citizen. His unique way of coping with hearing and speaking English instead of his native Arabic seems to have been to write these poems – as an autobiography-in-verse. They capture and embody so many personal, fresh, amusing, sad, astute and even disorienting resonances, and at the same time are elegant, sonorous and easy on the ear when recited. Now teaching Arabic at the University of Pennsylvania, Almallah said about this collection: "I exiled myself into English, into a language I am not that comfortable with." We wait impatiently for his second collection, whether in English or Arabic. University of Chicago Press, September 2019. ISBN: 978-0226642642. Pbk, 96 pages, $18.00 / £14.00. E-book ISBN: 978-0226642789, $10.00 to $18.00 / £12/11.

Baghdad, Adieu, Selected Poems of Memory and Exile by Salah Al Hamdani. Translated from the French and introduced by Sonia Alland, the collection gathers thirty-five years of the Iraqi poet's works, from his first volume in Arabic, *Memory of Embers* (1983), to his latest collection, written originally in French, *For You I Dream* (2015). This is a substantial overview of his work, with the theme of exile "never far from his thoughts", changing as time goes by. As Sonia Alland says in her introduction: "the young poet dreams of return; the older, wiser poet, recently a grandfather, has achieved the understanding that comes with age and experience – the realisation that there is no home to which he can return". Seagull Press, January 2019. ISBN: 978-0857425447. Hbk, 264 pages, $24.50 / £18.99.

The Trace of a Smile is a chapbook collection of 19 selected poems by Moroccan poet and translator Mbarek Sryfi, who is described by Eric Sellin as 'best imagined as the proverbial unnoticed "fly on the wall", but one now caught up in the web of life'. Each poem is a lyrical observation of a "human landscape", either of a moment out and about in a street, in a coffee bar, in a shop, seeing a beggar smile, passing a destitute mother and child (both in PJs), or a thoughtful reflection on age, on being a stranger, on escaping war, on time and life passing by. The collection took first place in the 2018 Moonstone Arts Center's Annual Chapbook Contest. Moonstone Press, Philadelphia, 2018. ISBN: 978-19461450806. Chapbook, 26 pages, $10.00.

CONTRIBUTORS

Ahmad Abdulatif (b.1978) is a novelist, translator, journalist, and researcher from Cairo. He has published six novels: *The Keymaker* (2010), winner of the State Incentive Award for Literature; *The Book of the Sculptor* (2013), which won first prize in the 2015 Sawiris Award for best novel by an emerging writer ; *Elias* (2014), a critically acclaimed work hailed as "a novel which lays the foundations of a new Arabic prose"; *Fortress of Dust* (2017), longlisted for the 2018 International Prize for Arabic Fiction and translated into Spanish; *Legs That Know Unprompted When To Leave* (2019). Numerous critical studies have discussed Abdulatif's work, including Amani Fouad's *The Novel and Society* and *The Anti-Novel* by Dr. Mohammed Mishbal.

Hassan Abdulrazzak is of Iraqi origin, born in Prague and living in London. A playwright, essayist and poet, he holds a PhD in molecular biology and has worked at Harvard and Imperial College. His plays include *And Here I Am, Trump in Palestine, Baghdad Wedding, The Prophet*, and *Love, Bombs & Apples*. He has been commissioned to write a number of plays, including *Dhow Under The Sun*, and *Catalina* and is currently working on a number of theatre, TV and film projects.

Samer Abu Hawwash is a poet and literary translator, born in Lebanon to a family of Palestinian refugees. His first collection of poetry (in Arabic), *Life is Printed in New York*, was published in 1997. Since then he has published nine poetry collections, including *This is Not the Way to Make Pizza*, plus two novels (2004 and 2005). He has translated into Arabic the poetry of more than twenty American poets, and more than forty fiction and non-fiction works of major American writers.

Monir Almajid was born in 1951 in Qamishli, Syria. He graduated from Damascus University in the Faculty of Fine Arts, and since 1969 has been a film critic, writing for Syrian and Arab media. After settling in Denmark in 1983, in 2008 he became editor of the Danish newspaper *Al Khabar*. His first novel, *Qamishlo*, was excerpted in *Banipal 56* (2016).

Abdelkader Benali is a Moroccan-Dutch writer and journalist, born in 1975 in Ighazzazen, Morocco. His family, of Berber background, migrated to the Netherlands when he was four and settled in Rotterdam. His debut novel *Bruiloft aan zee* (Wedding by the Sea) was a huge success and translated into many languages. He received the Libris Prize for his second novel, *De langverwachte* (The Long-Awaited). He has also written articles and reviews in Dutch newspapers. An avid long-distance runner wrote a book about his failed attempt to improve his best result, *Marathonloper* (Marathon Runner).

Abbas Beydoun is a poet and novelist, born in Tyre, Southern Lebanon, in 1945 to a family passionate about literature. He studied Arabic Literature in Beirut's Arab University, and achieved his MA in Literature from the Sorbonne, France. He has published numerous poetry collections, and in 2002, his first novel, *Blood Test* (Syracuse University Press, 2008 trans. Max Weiss), followed by two further works and his novel *Autumn of Innocence*, excerpted above, which won the 2017 Sheikh Zayed Book Award for Literature.

Raphael Cohen is a translator based in Cairo and is a *Banipal* contributing editor. He has translated novels by Mona Prince, Ahlam Mosteghanemi, Eslam Mosbah, George Yaraq and Mohamed Salmawy.

Fadia Faqir was born in Amman, Jordan, in 1956. Since 1990 she has published four novels, *Nisanit, Pillars of Salt,* and *My Name is Salma* and *Willow Trees Don't Weep*, which have been published in 19 countries and translated into 15 languages. She has the first PhD in Critical and Creative Writing in the UK from University of East Anglia and is currently a Fellow of St Aidan's College, Durham University, teaching Creative Writing.

Linda France is a poet, tutor, editor and mentor, teaching Creative Writing at Newcastle University. She is based near Hadrian's Wall in Northumberland and is pursuing her PhD on Women and Landscape. She studied English and History at Leeds University, and lived

CONTRIBUTORS

in London and Amsterdam before returning to the UK's North East.

Yasmeen Hanoosh is a bilingual Iraqi scholar, writer and translator who works across languages and genres. She is the author of *The Chaldeans: Politics and Identity in Iraq and the American Diaspora* (I.B. Tauris, 2019). Her Arabic stories have appeared in *Kikah Magazine*, while her English translations have appeared in literary journals, including *Banipal*, *World Literature Today*, and *The Iowa Review*. She is the translator of Luay Hamza Abbas's *Closing His Eyes* (National Endowment for the Arts Award, 2010) and Muhsin al-Ramli's *Scattered* (Arkansas Arabic Manuscript Translation Prize, 2002).

Becky Harrison is the Events and Communications Officer at the Arab British Centre in London. She has an MA in Comparative Cultural Analysis (University of Amsterdam), and a BA in Cultural Studies (Leeds).

William Maynard Hutchins has translated many contemporary Arab authors including Naguib Mahfouz. He was joint-winner of the 2013 Saif Ghobash Banipal Prize for *A Land Without Jasmine* by Wajdi al-Ahdal (Garnet, 2012) and won ALTA's 2015 NTA for Ibrahim al-Koni's *New Waw*. His most recent work is al-Koni's *The Fetishists*.

Suzanne Heukensfeldt Jansen was born and lived in the Netherlands until the age of 18 when she moved to London to study drama. Whilst in college, she was approached for her first translation job: translating Dutch comic strips for Marvel Comics. She become a full-time Dutch-English language specialist after gaining her (CIOL) Diploma in Translation in 1989, the year it was launched.

Abdel Aziz Jassim was born in Ras al-Khaimah, UAE, in 1962. He has published his poetry and literary articles since the early 1980s, and has four poetry collections and a book of essays, with selected poems translated into English, French and German. In 2017, part one of his collected works was published by Dar al-Tanweer, Beirut.

Samira Kawar is an experienced energy journalist and literary translator. She has translated for Banipal since it started, and is a trustee of the Banipal Trust for Arab Literature. She has translated novels by Liana Badr and Abdul Rahman Munif.

Said Khatibi, born in 1984 in Bou Saada, Algeria. He has worked as a cultural journalist since 2006, and writes in both Arabic and French. His Arabic works include *The Book of Sins* (2013), *The inflamed Gardens of the East* (2015) excerpted above, *Forty Years Waiting for Isabelle* (2016) for which he won the Katara Award for the Novel, and *Sarajevo's Firewood* (2018). His translations include Kateb Yacine's poetry collection *Loin de Nedjma*.

Khaled Al-Masri is Associate Professor of Arabic, Swarthmore College (PA, USA). He earned his PhD in Near Eastern Studies from the University of Michigan, Ann Arbor and his MA and BA in Arabic Language and Literature from Yarmouk University, Irbid, Jordan. He has translated two books from Arabic into English and is a regular translator for *Banipal*. His academic interests include 20th-century Arabic literature, gender studies, war narratives, migrant and refugee literature, and literary and translation theory.

Robin Moger is a translator, living in Cape Town, South Africa. He won the 2017 Saif Ghobash Banipal Prize for *The Book of Safety* by Yasser Abdel Hafez (Hoopoe Fiction, 2016). His translation of Hoda Barakat's *The Night Post* is forthcoming

Hassouna Mosbahi is a Tunisian writer, literary critic and journalist, born in Kairouan. He lived and worked in Munich, Germany, from 1985 to 2005. He won the National Novel Prize (Tunisia) in 1986, the Munich Tukan Prize for the German translation of his novel *Tarshish Hallucination* in 2000, and in 2016 the Mohamed Zefzef Prize, awarded by the Moroccan Assilah Forum. He has published four volumes of short stories, six novels, a travel book and some non-fiction. *A Tunisian Tale* (AUC Press, 2011) is his first novel in English translation and his latest novel is *We Don't Swim in the River Twice* (2019).

CONTRIBUTORS

Clare Roberts has a BA in Arabic and Islamic Studies from Oxford University, and an MA in Arabic Poetry and Turkish Politics from SOAS, London). She works at Gingko Library and is a contributing editor of Banipal and a regular reviewer.

Nancy Roberts has translated many works by Arab authors, including Naguib Mahfouz, Salwa Bakr, Mohamed el-Bisatie, Ezzat el Kamhawi and Hala El-Badry, also Ghada Samman, Laila Aljohani, Ahlem Mosteghanemi, and Ibrahim Nasrallah. She was awarded the 2018 Sheikh Hamad Translation Award for her translation of Ibrahim Nasrallah's *Gaza Weddings*.

Shadi Rohana, born in Haifa in 1985, is a Palestinian academic and literary translator based in México City, translating between Arabic, Spanish and English. He has introduced and translated a number of Latin American authors from Spanish to Arabic, as well as speeches and declarations from the EZLN in Chiapas. The Arabic translation of José Emilio Pacheco's *Las batallas en el desierto* (Palestine, 2016) was his first novel-length work.

Chip Rossetti has translated several works of Arabic fiction, including *Beirut, Beirut* by Sonallah Ibrahim, *Utopia* by Ahmed Khaled Towfik, and the graphic novel *Metro* by Magdy El Shafee. He is Editorial Director of the Library of Arabic Literature

Paul Starkey is an award-winning translator and Emeritus Professor of Arabic at Durham University and a contributing editor of Banipal. Recent translations include *Praise for the Women of the Family* by Mahmoud Shukair (shortlisted for the 2016 IPAF) and *The Shell* by Mustafa Khalifa, for which he was awarded the 2017 Sheikh Hamad

Stephanie Petit studied Linguistics at SOAS University of London. Since 2017, she has worked as a Digital Archivist in the Endangered Languages Archive, SOAS, where, among other things, she maintains digital collections of Modern South Arabian.

Hannah Somerville is a London-based investigative journalist and former health reporter. She has a BA in Arabic and Spanish from the University of Leeds and an MA in Arabic Literature from SOAS, University of London. Her dissertation focused on body politics in new Egyptian 'dystopian' fiction.

Adam Talib, DPhil (2014) Oxford, teaches Arabic language and literature at Durham University and is an assistant editor of the Journal of Arabic Literature. Before joining Durham, he taught at the American University in Cairo from 2012-2017

Susannah Tarbush is a freelance journalist specialising in Middle Eastern cultural affairs. She writes the Tanjara blog, and is a consulting editor of *Banipal* and regular reviewer.

Abdo Wazen is a Lebanese poet, translator and author of many collections of poetry, translations, novels and critical essays. He has worked as a cultural journalist in Beirut since 1979 and is currently cultural editor of the *Independent Arabia* online newspaper.

Jonathan Wright is an award-winning translator of fiction by Arab authors, including Mazen Maarouf, Ahmed Saadawi, Hassan Blasim, Saud Alsanousi, Youssef Ziedan and Khaled el-Khamissi.

Farouk Yousif (b. 1955) is a poet and art critic, from Baghdad, Iraq. He studied Art at the Baghdad Academy of Fine Art and published his first collection of poems, *Silent Songs*, in 1996. Since then he has published six further collections of poetry, five books of art criticism and six travelogues. In 2006, he won the Ibn Battuta Award for Travel Literature for *Nothing Nobody*. He lives in London and writes for *Al-Arab* newspaper.

Kafa Al-Zou'bi: Please see the feature on her above, pages 144-175

For more information on all the authors in *Banipal 66*
and all the translators, writers and book reviewers, please go to:
www.banipal.co.uk/contributors/